# The Book On Uncertainty

## Why We Crave Control, and How to Let Go

### The Book On Series

## Oliver Bennett

Published by The Book On Publishing, 2025.
First edition. July 28, 2025.

I0458770

Website: https://thebookon.ca
Substack: https://thebookonpublishing.substack.com/

While every precaution has been taken in the preparation of this book, the publisher assumes no responsibility for errors or omissions, or damages resulting from the use of the information contained herein.

The Book On Uncertainty: Why We Crave Control, and How to Let Go

**First edition. July 28, 2025.**

Copyright © 2025 The Book On Publishing
ISBN: 978-1-997795-78-0

Written by Oliver Bennett

# The Book On Series

The Book On Life Unscripted

The Book On Risk Management in Payments

The Book On AI for Everyday People

The Book On Relationships

The Book On Master The Algorithm

The Book On Saying No

The Book On Community Led Strategy

The Book On The Myth of Multitasking

The Book On The Burnout Blueprint

The Book On The Digital Reboot

The Book On The Shape of What's Coming

The Book On Strategic Obsession

The Book On High-Stakes Thinking

The Book On Artificial Leverage

The Book On Clarity

The Book On Uncertainty

The Book On Operational Excellence

The Book On Escape

# Read This First

This is not a book designed to entertain you. It's not here to charm, to soothe, or to hold your hand. It won't dazzle you with stories, metaphors, or motivational fluff. What you're having is a tool, an instruction manual written for people who are serious about learning, executing, and thinking at a higher level.

Every book in The Book On Series is built on a single premise: clarity beats complexity. We believe that when you strip away the noise, the emotions, the marketing spin, and the cultural rituals of "self-help," what's left is raw, unembellished instruction. That's what these books offer.

They are dry by design. Not because we don't care about language or narrative, but because when you're building something that matters, you don't need more distractions. You need a clear architecture. Mental scaffolding. Direction that respects your intelligence.

Each title in this series takes on a specific domain: decision-making, clarity, strategy, leverage, and uncertainty, and drills deep, not in sweeping generalizations, but in applied frameworks. These are books for builders, operators, founders, tacticians, and thinkers—people who don't just consume knowledge but operationalize it.

You'll find no chapter-long anecdotes here. No self-congratulatory memoirs. No bullet-point platitudes. Instead, what you'll get is structured insight: argument, example, application. The tone is direct. The prose is sober. The ideas are designed to be lifted out and used.

You won't be coddled, but you won't be misled either.

There's a place in the world for lyrical, emotional, story-driven books, and this isn't that place. This is a workspace. A blueprint. A conversation for people who are ready to act, not just absorb.

We respect your time and your intellect.

Welcome to The Book On Series.

# Table of Contents

# Dedication

To those who face the unknown with open eyes and restless hearts, may this book be a companion on your journey through the fog. To the seekers who dare to pause, to question, and to move forward without certainty, this is for you. And to everyone who understands that courage is not the absence of fear, but the choice to live fully despite it.

May you find strength in the stillness, clarity in the chaos, and freedom in the unfolding.

- Oliver

# Acknowledgments

This book could not have been written without the generous support, wisdom, and encouragement of many people who have journeyed with me through the fog of uncertainty.

To my family and close friends: thank you for your patience and faith when the path was unclear and the questions loomed large. Your presence grounded me more than words can express.

To the mentors and teachers who modeled courage in complexity, your lessons echo throughout these pages. You showed me that uncertainty is not an obstacle but an invitation.

To the readers who have trusted my voice across previous works and welcomed this one with open minds and hearts, your curiosity and critical engagement inspire me to keep refining and pushing forward.

To the countless conversations, both problematic and illuminating, that challenged me to look deeper, feel more honestly, and write with greater clarity, these dialogues were the true crucible of this work.

And finally, to every person navigating their uncertainty, wrestling with fear, and choosing to move forward anyway, this book is for you. May it serve as a companion and a reminder that you are not alone.

# Prologue

## The Tide Before the Wave

Uncertainty is not just a condition we endure; it's the undercurrent that shapes every decision, every moment, every breath. Yet, we live as though certainty were the default, as though the future could be tamed, predicted, controlled. We cast plans like anchors, seeking safe harbors in a sea that refuses to stay still.

But the truth is this: uncertainty is the tide before the wave. It is the shifting wind that fills the sails. It is the space where creation happens, not despite chaos, but because of it.

I've spent years watching how people respond to uncertainty. How we crave control, how we freeze, how we fight, and sometimes how we learn to surf instead. This book is about that dance, the art of living when the map dissolves beneath your feet, when the only constant is change.

You won't find formulas here. No guarantees. No checklist to tick off. Instead, you'll find stories, reflections, and strategies rooted in the messy reality of life as it is, unpredictable, uncomfortable, and profoundly transformative.

If you're reading this, it's likely because you've felt the sting of uncertainty. Maybe it's a decision hanging over you, a fear lurking beneath your confidence, or a sense that the world is moving faster than you can keep up with. You're not alone.

This book isn't about conquering uncertainty; it's about understanding and embracing it. It teaches how to flow with uncertainty instead of resisting it. It's about cultivating resilience, not by fleeing from fear, but by accepting it as a constant companion on the journey. The tide is rising; the wave is coming. Will you learn to surf?

## Chapter 1: The Certainty Addiction

I used to think I was good at planning. Friends would ask how I always seemed to stay calm under pressure, how I never got caught off guard. What I didn't tell them was that I wasn't quiet, I was compulsive. I had a spreadsheet for everything. I ran mental simulations for the worst-case scenario of every trip, project, and conversation. I didn't just anticipate problems; I rehearsed failure like it was a role I might someday be cast in. If something bad were going to happen, at least I wanted the illusion that I'd seen it coming.

What I mistook for preparedness was, in hindsight, a kind of addiction, not to knowledge, but to the appearance of control. And like all addictions, it offered a short-term fix at the cost of long-term clarity. I wasn't more in control of my life; I was more reactive, more anxious, more desperate to avoid discomfort. Planning became a drug. And certainty, or the fantasy of it, was my dealer.

The truth is, we're all a little addicted to certainty. We crave it not because it's useful, but because it's soothing. Certainty is the emotional equivalent of gravity; it grounds us, even when the ground is a lie. The moment we feel unsure, our brains start racing to construct some explanation, any explanation, that can return us to the illusion of stability. We call this clarity, but really, it's often just closure in disguise.

I started noticing this everywhere once I knew what to look for. A friend stayed in a toxic relationship not because she believed it would get better, but because the pain was familiar. A predictable hell is often more comforting than an unpredictable purgatory. Another friend turned down a job that would have challenged him to grow, simply because the ambiguity of a new city, a new routine, felt intolerable. He told himself it wasn't "the right fit," but I could see what he was saying: *I don't know what will happen, and I hate that.*

We build our lives around rituals of certainty. We map out our five-year plans. We obsess over productivity tools. We scroll endlessly for the "right" opinion, the definitive podcast, the one hot take that will make the messy world make sense. Entire industries thrive on this hunger. Forecasting. Insurance. Personal finance. Self-help. Religion. Algorithms. They all sell the same thing, dressed in different clothes: predictability. A future that feels like it can be controlled, or at least correctly guessed.

But here's the thing. The more certain we try to become, the more rigid we get. And the more rigid we get, the more brittle we become when the world doesn't cooperate. The very thing we hope will keep us safe and in control is often what makes us most vulnerable when reality veers off script.

I learned this the hard way. It was a time in my life when everything should have been going well. I had just finished a significant project, one I thought would open doors. I had money in the bank, clients lined up, and a clean bill of health. On paper, everything looked stable. But then, in two months, three unplanned events cracked that paper-thin sense of order wide open: my partner's job fell through, my father had a stroke, and a tech platform I relied on to deliver client work went dark with no warning and no recovery plan.

I'd love to tell you I handled it with grace. I didn't. I scrambled. I raged. I blamed myself for not foreseeing the unforeseeable. And then I did what every certainty addict does in withdrawal: I tried to *fix* the chaos by doubling down on control. I redid my budget. I built redundancies. I called five mentors to ask what they would do. I came up with a new plan to replace the old one. And none of it helped, because the problem wasn't that I had failed to anticipate. The problem was that I believed I *could.*

That belief, that certainty is achievable if we try hard enough, is the addiction we rarely name. It hides behind ambition. It hides behind excellence. It even hides behind virtue. But it's an illusion that quietly robs us of the very thing we need most in an unpredictable world: adaptability.

There's a kind of spiritual violence we do to ourselves when we demand certainty from a world that never promised it. We start thinking that uncertainty is a sign of failure rather than a feature of reality. We believe our confusion indicates that we haven't conducted sufficient research, or that our discomfort suggests we're on the wrong path. We pivot endlessly, grasping for the next fix. We don't trust our judgment, because judgment doesn't feel as secure as certainty. We want facts, not feelings. We want maps, not instincts. We want formulas, not frameworks. And we don't want to admit that we might have to make crucial decisions with incomplete information.

But that's precisely what life is—a series of bets placed in the fog. No matter how much you prepare, the mist never fully lifts. It just shifts, and sometimes you get a break in the clouds. Other times, you move forward blind.

If I could go back and talk to my younger self, the one clinging to plans like a drowning man clings to driftwood, I wouldn't tell him to stop planning. I'd say to him to prepare differently. To see his maps not as guarantees, but as guesses. I'd say to him that resilience doesn't come from being right, it comes from being ready to be wrong and still keep going. I'd tell him that it's okay not to know. That not knowing isn't a weakness. It's the beginning of wisdom.

Certainty feels safe. But safety isn't the same as sanity. When we cling too tightly to what we *think* we know, we become less capable of seeing what's happening. We filter out information that contradicts our mental models. We ignore signals that don't fit the story we're telling ourselves. And we resist change, not because change is bad, but because it threatens the illusion we've built our identities around.

So this book begins here: with the admission that we are all, to some degree, recovering certainty addicts. Not because we're weak, but because we've been trained to believe the unknown is dangerous. In truth, it's just unfamiliar. And the unfamiliar, while uncomfortable, is also where life happens. Growth, love, opportunity, invention, all of it lives beyond the edge of certainty.

The goal, then, is not to eliminate uncertainty. That's impossible. The goal is to build a life where uncertainty is not a threat, but a terrain. A place we know how to walk through. A place we don't have to fear.

This book is my map of that terrain. But it is not a perfect map. It will not give you answers. It will not eliminate doubt. What it might do, if we're lucky, is help you stop needing perfect answers in the first place. It might help you surf, instead of sink.

# Chapter 2: The Insecurity Beneath Order

Order is a performance. A tidy kitchen, a color-coded calendar, a well-pressed shirt- these are all signals. They say, "I've got this." They say, "I'm in control." They whisper competence in a world that's always watching for cracks. But if you stand still long enough, if you pay attention, you start to feel the tension buzzing under all that neatness. Order, for many of us, is not the goal; it's the mask. And underneath it, there's often a quiet, unspoken panic.

I started noticing this years ago, when I found myself fixating on things that didn't matter. I'd reorganize my workspace for the third time in a week. I'd spend half an hour deciding the "right" productivity app for a project I hadn't even started. I'd delay writing by insisting I needed a better writing environment. It all looked industrious on the surface. But none of it was about doing the work. It was about managing the anxiety that comes with the work. The fear of starting, of failing, of not knowing what might happen once the thing left the safety of my mind and entered the real, unpredictable world.

This isn't unique to me. I've seen it in people across every field. The executive who over-prepares for meetings to avoid improvisation. The writer who rewrites the first paragraph fifty times and never gets to the second. The friend who plans every vacation down to the minute because the idea of "just seeing what happens" triggers something profound and old. We use order like a charm to ward off chaos, but what we're trying to manage is our fear of exposure.

I've come to believe that much of what we call "high functioning" is just well-disguised insecurity. We praise those who are punctual, precise, and relentless, but we rarely ask what drives them. Sometimes it's discipline. Often, it's dread. Dread of being seen as incompetent. Dread of being surprised. Dread of being vulnerable in a world that punishes anything that looks like weakness.

I remember a conversation I had with a surgeon once. Brilliant guy. Steady hands, high success rate, revered in his field. But off the record, after a few drinks, he admitted that he didn't sleep the night before complicated procedures. Not because he wasn't prepared, he was always overprepared. But because he couldn't stand the idea that some variable, some unknowable thing, might show up mid-operation and remind him that even his expertise had limits. He said it felt like standing on the edge of a cliff and praying the ground doesn't shift. And so he created rituals, morning habits, lucky pens, music cues, not because they had any actual power, but because they made the fear tolerable.

We all have our versions of this. The things we do to make uncertainty feel manageable. Some of us make lists. Some of us make rules. Some of us rehearse conversations in our heads a dozen times before making a call. All of it comes from the same root: a discomfort with not knowing, and the desperate hope that maybe, just maybe, if we're orderly enough, the world will leave us alone.

But of course, it never does.

The world, for all our efforts to contain it, refuses to behave. Children get sick—markets tank. People betray. Projects implode. Technology fails. And when that happens, when the system we built to protect ourselves gets shaken, the real question surfaces: what were we protecting all along?

The answer, more often than not, is identity—the image we hold of ourselves. I'm the competent one. I'm the steady one. I'm the one who doesn't panic. These stories become anchors, but they also become cages. We get invested in being seen a certain way that we can't afford to admit, even to ourselves, that we're scared, or lost, or unsure. Instead of acknowledging the fear, we double down on order. We organize, optimize, and perfect. Not because it makes things better, but because it keeps the mask intact.

There's nothing wrong with order. Systems are useful. Routines can be life-saving. But they are only healthy when they serve us, not when they silence us. When order becomes a coping mechanism rather than a tool, it starts to rot. It calcifies. And over time, it stops helping us navigate uncertainty and starts making us more brittle in the face of it.

I've watched entire teams fall apart not because their systems failed, but because their identities were too fragile to handle disruption. The leader who needs to be right can't admit when the plan isn't working. The analyst who prides herself on accuracy becomes defensive when asked to work with incomplete data. The creative who built his brand on originality shuts down when trends shift and his old instincts stop landing. In each case, the problem isn't the uncertainty; it's the inability to metabolize it.

And yet, the irony is that uncertainty doesn't always destroy us. Sometimes it reveals us. It strips away the scripts, the costumes, the clever little frameworks we've been hiding behind. It leaves us naked. And in that nakedness, if we're honest, we start to see what we were terrified of: not the chaos itself, but what it might expose about who we are without our usual armor.

I had a client once, a startup founder, who came to me after his second product launch had flopped. He was angry, but underneath the anger, I could see the fear. Not fear of failure, but fear of irrelevance. His whole identity was built on being a visionary, a disruptor. And now, the market was shrugging at his big idea. His first instinct was to blame the timing, the messaging, the product-market fit. But as we talked, it became clear that what was bothering him was that he didn't know what to do next, and he had no internal script for "not knowing."

We worked together not on strategy, but on tolerance. Tolerance for ambiguity. Tolerance for silence. Tolerance for having to sit in a room and not having an answer yet. It was excruciating for him. But slowly, as he stopped trying to fix everything, he started listening better. To his team. To the data. To himself. And eventually, something cracked open. Not a breakthrough idea, those come later, but a kind of internal spaciousness. The realization that his value wasn't in always having a plan. It was in being able to stay with the question longer than most people are willing to.

That's what most of us need, not more order, but more capacity. More room inside ourselves for the unknown. More willingness to say "I don't know yet" without feeling like an impostor. More comfort with the fact that life does not come with a clean interface or a guaranteed response time. It arrives in a messy state, out of sequence, and often without instructions. And the best we can do is stay present long enough to understand what it's asking of us.

So when I catch myself reaching for some illusion of control, another list, another plan, another perfectly curated response, I try to pause. I try to ask what I'm running from. Nine times out of ten, it's not the task I'm avoiding. It's the uncertainty embedded inside it. The possibility that I might not be who I think I am if I can't master this moment. And that's the truth at the core of this chapter: our addiction to order isn't really about the world being unpredictable. It's about our fear of what that unpredictability might reveal about us.

But here's the question: what if the exposure isn't the danger we think it is? What if letting go of the mask, even briefly, is the first step toward being someone not who *knows*, but who *notices*? Someone who isn't obsessed with appearing ready, but is open enough to respond.

That kind of presence is not clean. It's not impressive. But it is, I think, the beginning of absolute power. Because once we stop outsourcing our security to the structure of things, we begin to source it from within. And that kind of security, quiet, internal, flexible, can't be taken by circumstance. It can only be grown.

# Chapter 3: Nostalgia for a Past That Never Was

There's a peculiar trick the mind plays when the present feels unstable: it romanticizes the past. We don't even notice it happening most of the time. One moment, we're frustrated with how complicated everything feels, and the next, we're staring wistfully into the rearview mirror, sure that things used to be simpler, better, and more certain. We talk about "the good old days" as if they were a fixed point in history. But the more I've examined that impulse in myself, the more I've come to realize: what I was longing for wasn't the past. It was a fantasy. A cleaned-up, heavily edited highlight reel that only exists because I'm terrified of the chaos right in front of me.

I used to do this all the time. In the middle of some personal or professional mess, when a project stalled, or a relationship got difficult, or the news cycle felt unbearable, I'd drift into memory like it was a safe room. I'd think about the years when I felt more confident, more capable, more secure. Sometimes I'd go further back to childhood summers where the days stretched out endlessly and the only uncertainty was whether the ice cream truck would come before dinner.

It felt comforting. But it was also a lie.

Because those times weren't free of uncertainty, I didn't recognize it. Or maybe I didn't have to carry it myself. Someone else was managing the ambiguity, the adults, the systems, the scaffolding around me. And even then, things weren't as stable as I now imagine. The friendships were fragile. The finances were tight. The world was still spinning out behind the curtain. I didn't have the eyes to see it.

21

That's what nostalgia does. It flattens the past into something easier to digest. It removes the noise, the doubt, the mess. It gives us a version of life with clean edges and clear outcomes. But when we compare that polished memory to the raw, unsorted chaos of the present, it's not a fair fight. The present always loses. Because now, we're too aware. Too responsible. Too exposed. We feel every ambiguity in high definition. And the more uncertain the now feels, the more we crave the illusion that things used to make sense.

This isn't just personal, it's cultural. Look around and you'll see a deep, widespread ache for imagined certainties. Politicians promise a return to greatness. Marketers sell us products that evoke memories of our childhood. Media companies reboot old shows, remake old movies, and repackage old music. And we eat it up, because it scratches the itch. It tells us that the past was knowable, controllable, and meaningful. That we used to understand the world, and maybe we can again, if we go back far enough.

But the past wasn't simpler. We were just less tangled in it. And longing for its false clarity does something dangerous: it steals our capacity to engage with the complexity in front of us. It makes us passive. It makes us yearn instead of act. We start to believe that the best has already happened, and that all we can do now is preserve what's left.

That mindset is a form of paralysis.

I remember meeting someone at a dinner party once, a man in his late sixties, who said, almost proudly, that he stopped keeping up with the world after 2008. "Everything's been downhill since then," he told me, swirling the ice in his glass. He listed all the reasons: technology made people antisocial, politics became a circus, music lost its soul, and attention spans vanished. "Back in my day," he said, "you knew where you stood."

I asked him what year he thought we should return to, if we could. He paused. "Probably 1985. Things felt right then."

I didn't push it in the moment, but later I thought about what 1985 held. The Cold War. The AIDS crisis. Massive economic disparity. Political corruption. The seeds of everything we now call "broken" were already in full bloom. But for him, 1985 was the year before his divorce, before his industry collapsed, before the world demanded that he adapt in ways he didn't want to.

So that's what he meant. Not that 1985 was perfect. But that *he* was.

That's the real pull of nostalgia, not toward a better world, but toward a more stable self. When we say we miss how things used to be, what we often mean is that we forget who we were when we didn't feel so lost. We miss the version of ourselves that wasn't yet tested by this level of uncertainty. And rather than face the discomfort of reinvention, we cling to the identities that once felt firm.

But the world changes. It always has. And when we refuse to meet it where it is, when we idealize a past that never really existed, we rob ourselves of the power to shape anything new.

This shows up in smaller ways, too. In teams that keep using broken processes because "that's how we've always done it." In people who stay in expired relationships because "it used to feel right." In creatives who keep chasing the one formula that once worked, instead of asking what the moment is calling for now. All of it rooted in fear. The fear that if we stop clinging to what was, we'll have nothing solid left to stand on.

But sometimes, the solidity is the problem. It keeps us from moving. It keeps us from asking better questions. It keeps us from acknowledging that the world might now require something else from us, something unfamiliar, something unproven, something not yet clear.

I'm not immune to this. There are days I still pine for the simplicity of earlier versions of myself. Times when I had fewer responsibilities. When everything felt more linear. When I thought I could predict the shape of the following year. But then I remember: those were also the years I was most afraid of disruption. I didn't call it fear, I called it focus. I called it a drive. I called it discipline. But underneath all the ambition was a tightness, a rigidity, a refusal to let life be life.

And life, as I've learned the hard way, is not particularly interested in our fantasies of stability. It keeps evolving, whether we're ready or not. The question isn't whether things were better. The question is whether we're willing to live where we are.

There's a different kind of memory that I've started practicing. Not nostalgia, but recollection. I try to remember things as they were, not as I wish they were. I revisit difficult years and try to see the nuance. The times I thought I was thriving but was hiding. The times I felt lost, I was growing. The moments that were uncertain and terrifying and yet somehow led to breakthroughs I couldn't have orchestrated.

That's the strange gift of uncertainty; it often gives us more than we would have asked for. Not what we *want*, exactly, but what we *need* to evolve. It's uncomfortable, yes. But so is strength training. So is growth. So is truth.

When I feel myself drifting into the warm bath of "things used to be better," I try to pause. I try to ask: am I remembering, or am I escaping? Am I telling the truth, or am I soothing myself with fiction? And most importantly, what part of me is asking to be held right now, not with fantasy, but with presence?

Because if we're going to navigate this world honestly, we can't afford to mythologize the past. We need all our attention here. On this version of life. This version of ourselves. Imperfect, unresolved, uncertain, and alive.

## Chapter 4: False Maps and Broken Compasses

We are creatures of orientation. Give us a direction, a line to follow, even a myth to believe in, and we'll move. Take that away, and we freeze. Disoriented. Uncertain. Vulnerable. It's no surprise that over time, we've built maps, mental ones, social ones, ideological ones, to tell us where we are and what things mean. But the trouble with maps is that they're not the territory. And when we mistake the two, we get lost without realizing it.

I've used a lot of maps in my life: models, frameworks, principles, and belief systems. I've clung to them in the way a child clings to the edge of a swimming pool, grateful for structure, terrified of the unknown depth just inches away. Some of those maps were useful for a while. They helped me make sense of complexity, gave me traction when everything felt slippery. But over time, I began to notice that I wasn't questioning the map anymore. I was trying to force my experience to fit inside it.

There was a period when I became obsessed with productivity systems. You know the type: GTD, time blocking, Pomodoro, Eisenhower matrix, task triage by energy level. I devoured them like sacred texts. Not because I was inefficient, but because I felt overwhelmed and thought the right system would save me. And for a while, it did. But eventually I noticed a strange inversion: I wasn't using the system, it was using me. The map had become the terrain. And when something didn't fit neatly into the structure, I felt like I was failing, not the model.

That's the danger of false maps. They start as tools and quietly become idols.

And it's not just systems. I've followed maps handed down through culture, too. The one that says success looks like a house, a family, a retirement plan. Or the one that says freedom means working for yourself. Or that love must follow a specific arc with specific milestones. I've tried to follow these maps, even when the compass in my gut was pointing somewhere else. Because to go off-map is to wander. And we don't like wanderers. We treat them as naïve, broken, or suspicious, as if the only safe way to live is to follow paths already paved by someone else.

But here's the thing about someone else's path: it wasn't built for your terrain.

I learned this the hard way when I tried to scale a business using someone else's playbook. I followed the "rules", target market analysis, conversion funnels, strategic partnerships, and automated engagement. It all looked good on paper. But it never quite worked. I kept tweaking things, trying to make them fit. At one point, I even wondered if I was the problem; maybe I wasn't executing well enough. But then a mentor said something that rattled me. He said, "You're not failing to implement a good strategy. You're succeeding at implementing the wrong one."

It stopped me cold.

I'd been trying to navigate with a map that didn't match my actual terrain, my values, my audience, my way of working. And no matter how detailed the instructions were, they kept taking me in circles. That's the curse of a false map: it gives you the confidence to move, but not the clarity to arrive.

Eventually, I had to step back and start asking more complex questions. What matters to me about this work? Who am I trying to serve? What kind of life am I building alongside this business?

The answers didn't point to any existing model. They pointed to something more ambiguous, something more challenging to monetize or define. But for the first time in months, I felt like I was facing the right direction, even if I didn't know the destination yet.

That's when I started thinking about compasses.

Maps are external. They show you where other people have gone. But compasses are internal. They point based on something more profound, your true north. And while they don't give you turn-by-turn directions, they keep you from walking in the wrong direction just because the road looks well-lit.

The problem is that most of us no longer trust our compasses. We've outsourced our orientation to the experts, the influencers, the algorithms. We wait for consensus before moving. We check what others are doing, then triangulate our own decisions from there. But in doing so, we become strangers to our instincts.

I've had to relearn how to feel my compass. It doesn't shout. It doesn't justify itself. It hums. It tightens when something is off. It softens when something aligns. It's not rational in the way spreadsheets are logical, but it's not irrational either. It's what you feel when you say, "This just isn't me" or "I don't know why, but this feels right."

For a long time, I ignored those signals. I thought being a grown-up meant overriding instinct in favor of logic. But logic, as it turns out, is only as good as the assumptions it rests on. And if those assumptions come from maps that no longer match your world, then all the logic in the world won't save you.

One of the most dangerous things a person can do in a world that's changing fast is to follow a map drawn for a world that no longer exists. We see this everywhere: in institutions that cling to outdated norms, in leaders who use old playbooks for new problems, and in individuals who try to force modern chaos into antique frames. And the more scared people become, the more tightly they cling to these old maps. Not because they work, but because they're familiar.

There's a tragic kind of comfort in a broken compass. At least it gives you something to hold. But the cost is high: disorientation, regret, inertia. You can end up years deep in the wrong life and not realize it until something forces you to stop.

What do we do?

We learn to navigate again.

We stop pretending that certainty is possible. We accept that most of life is not a straight road but a shifting field. We get better at listening to our internal signals. We learn to pause, recalibrate, question our maps, and sometimes even walk backwards. And most of all, we stop looking for one definitive system to save us. Because there isn't one. There never was.

The people I admire most are not the ones with the most impressive strategies. They're the ones who've developed the most honest relationship with uncertainty. They're the ones who can say, "I don't know where this leads, but it feels true," and still move. They're the ones who check their compass before their calendar. Who understands that knowing what's right is not the same as knowing what's next.

There's courage in that kind of navigation. It's quieter than bravado. It doesn't announce itself. But you can feel it in the room when someone is walking their line, not because it's easy, but because it's theirs.

So, here's what I hold now: maps are helpful. Compasses are essential. But you can't substitute one for the other. Know the difference. Update the map. Tune the compass. And when the two conflict, don't be afraid to trust what's more complicated to explain.

Because in the end, the path that belongs to you won't be the most visible. It won't always be efficient. It won't get the most applause. But it will be the one you can walk without abandoning yourself. And that's the only direction that matters.

## Chapter 5: When Planning Fails

There's a moment, usually quiet, often private, when you realize the plan isn't working. It's not always dramatic. Sometimes it's just a dull thud in your chest as you reread the schedule, the projections, the bullet points you wrote when everything still seemed clear. You look at the work, the effort, the logic behind it all, and it doesn't matter. The world has moved in a way the plan didn't account for. And there you are, frozen with your perfect plan in your hands, watching the water rise around you.

I've been there more times than I'd like to admit. There were times when I mapped everything out: the steps, the timelines, the contingencies. I ran scenarios in my head, set buffer zones, and padded expectations. I planned not just for success, but for resilience. And still, the plan failed. Not because I didn't plan well, but because the world refused to read my script.

There was one year in particular when this happened on every level. I had a book launch scheduled, tied to a speaking tour, tied to a product rollout. Everything was synchronized. I'd worked backward from every milestone like I was staging a military campaign. It wasn't just a plan; it was a system. A machine of intentions cross-checked and confirmed by people I trusted. And then, three days before the launch, a global event, unforeseen and unpreventable, stopped everything. The venues canceled. The rollout stalled. The promotion window evaporated. Just like that, months of careful orchestration collapsed.

At first, I did what most people do when a plan fails: I looked for salvage. What can I still use? What can I pivot? What angle will let me pretend this is just a minor adjustment, not a complete derailment? But as the hours turned into days and the uncertainty thickened, I had to face a more complicated truth: this wasn't a detour. The road was gone.

There's grief in that moment. No one talks about that part. We grieve not just the lost opportunity, but the version of ourselves that believed it could steer the outcome. We grieve the identity that was built into the plan: the visionary, the executor, the leader with foresight. And when the plan fails, it feels like *we* forget, as if competence and control were the same thing. As if effort guaranteed outcome. As if life were that linear.

But life isn't linear. It's not even directional sometimes. It loops, it jerks, it stalls. It contradicts itself. And while planning can help us feel prepared, it cannot insulate us from disruption. It was never supposed to. A plan is a guess, an educated one, maybe even a brilliant one, but a guess all the same.

We forget this because planning makes us feel secure. It's a ritual. A psychological ceremony we perform to calm the parts of us that are terrified of chaos. We plot out days, quarters, and years. We map our goals onto calendars, breaking them down into smaller, neater pieces, as if complexity can be tamed by slicing it thin enough. But the map, no matter how elegant, does not know the terrain. And often, the terrain doesn't care what we meant to happen.

I don't say this to dismiss planning. I still plan. I make outlines. I create timelines. I estimate resources. But I no longer confuse planning with control. I don't treat a plan as a contract with the universe. I treat it as scaffolding, something to help me get started, not something that guarantees I'll finish the way I imagined.

That shift didn't come easily. It came through failure. And through watching others around me buckle under the weight of their expectations. A friend of mine, a fellow entrepreneur, once confided in me that he'd rather *not start* a new initiative than risk having the plan go sideways. His logic was clean: better to preserve the idea than to expose it to the mess of reality. But underneath that logic was fear. Not of failure, exactly, but of humiliation. Of being seen making it up as he went. Because we're taught that success means confidence, foresight, and direction. No one tells you that half of progress is improvisation.

When planning fails, something deeper gets revealed: your ability to reorient. Not just to pivot, but to reassess the moment itself. To stop asking, "How do I get back on track?" and start asking, "What is the track now?" That's a more complicated question. It doesn't give you the emotional relief of continuing with momentum. It demands presence. It asks for humility. It invites creativity. And most terrifying of all, it requires you to move without a map for a while.

That's what I had to do in the aftermath of that failed launch. For weeks, I sat with the discomfort of unstructured time. I wanted to channel my energy into a new plan, to feel more grounded. But everything I tried felt premature. It wasn't until I allowed myself to observe without immediate fixes or replacement strategies that I began to see what was available. Not a new plan. A new context. The world had changed. And I needed to let go of my assumptions about what would work.

That space of "no plan" is one of the most uncomfortable, generative, and honest places I've ever been. It stripped me of my performative competence. It forced me to listen. It showed me who I was when I wasn't performing for anyone. And from that space, eventually, a new way of moving began to emerge, not based on salvaging the old plan, but on understanding what was now possible.

We're not taught to value that kind of uncertainty. We're taught to hide it, cover it, patch it with confidence. But if you talk to anyone who's built something enduring, an artist, an entrepreneur, a survivor, they'll tell you the same thing: there was a moment they had to throw the plan away. Not because they were weak, but because the plan was too small for the reality they were facing.

What they had to build instead was responsiveness.

That's the skill I've come to treasure. Not planning but responding. Not forcing clarity but making room for it to emerge. Not clinging to the vision but staying loyal to the deeper impulse behind it, even if it manifests differently than expected. That doesn't mean we abandon structure. It means we stop worshipping it.

When planning fails, what rises in its place is often quieter than we expect. A conversation you didn't think to schedule. An insight you wouldn't have had if everything had gone according to script. A collaboration that emerges because your original team fell apart. It doesn't come with a press release. It doesn't feel like triumph. It feels like emergence. Like something uninvited but somehow necessary showing up at your door.

We don't like that kind of arrival. We want to plan for good things. We want to know what's coming. But often, the best things come after we've let the old plan die.

So now, when I create a plan, I do it like a hiker sketching a route with a stick in the dirt, tentatively, provisionally, with the awareness that it might get washed away by the next rain. And when it does, I don't assume I've failed. I think the terrain is reminding me who's really in charge. And that maybe, just maybe, there's another way forward I wouldn't have seen if everything had gone according to plan.

# Chapter 6: Uncertainty in the Age of Optimization

There's a pressure humming underneath modern life, so constant we barely notice it anymore. It tells us to be better, more efficient, more productive, more optimized. We count steps, track sleep, and monitor heart rate variability. We optimize our inbox, workouts, nutrition, and calendars. Even our leisure time becomes a performance, curated and measured for maximum yield. The goal, we're told, is continuous improvement—no wasted motion. No slack. No ambiguity.

It sounds reasonable. Who doesn't want to be better? But over time, I've come to see that what we call "optimization" often has less to do with excellence and more to do with avoidance. We are not refining our lives to get closer to meaning. We are refining them to escape the discomfort of not knowing. Optimization has become the socially sanctioned armor we wear to defend ourselves against uncertainty.

I first noticed this in myself during a period when everything felt slightly off. Not broken, just brittle. I was sleeping enough, eating well, and producing steadily. From the outside, I was running like a well-oiled machine. But inside, I felt robotic. Hollow. It was as if I were living according to someone else's checklist. Every action had a metric. Every hour had a purpose. I'd optimized myself into a corner.

One morning, I caught myself reorganizing my reading list, not by subject or author, but by potential return on investment. Which books would yield the most professional insight per page? Which podcasts were worth the commute time? I was trying to hack curiosity. And in doing so, I realized something quietly devastating: I was no longer doing anything to *feel* something. I was doing everything to *produce* something.

That's what the age of optimization does to us. It turns life into an efficiency puzzle. It frames uncertainty not as a natural part of being human, but as a problem to be solved. Ambiguity becomes waste. Emotions become noise. Slowness becomes a bug in the system.

But life is not software.

You can't debug your way into meaning. You can't schedule your way around grief, or iterate your way out of heartbreak. You can't automate becoming. And yet that's precisely what we try to do when we treat ourselves like processes to be upgraded instead of people to be understood.

I've spoken with dozens of professionals who confess, often in whispers, that they're exhausted from chasing improvement. Not because they don't believe in growth, but because the kind of growth they're being sold never ends. There's always another metric, another app, another guru. Always a new way to "level up." And behind that constant push is a deep, gnawing fear: that if we ever stop optimizing, we'll fall behind. We'll become irrelevant. We'll be judged as lazy, disorganized, or undisciplined.

But maybe the real discipline is in knowing when to stop.

When to sit with an imperfect process. When to walk without tracking. When to write without outlining. When to live without optimizing.

That doesn't mean we abandon systems. It means we stop worshipping them.

I've come to believe that the most dangerous lie of the optimization age is that there is a "best" way to live. The idea is that with enough data, we can eliminate uncertainty. That if we tweak enough variables — input, output, behavior, mindset — we can finally arrive at the perfect routine, the ideal system, the perfect self.

But perfection is a mirage. And chasing it keeps us from experiencing the richness of imperfection.

I once worked with a client, a creative director, who was trying to reclaim his sense of vision after years in corporate strategy. He had every tool imaginable: AI-driven content planners, collaborative whiteboards, productivity dashboards. But when he sat down to create, he froze. "I've got everything dialed in," he said, "but I feel disconnected from the work."

We looked at his routine. It was airtight. Twenty-minute focus sprints. Calibrated music playlists. Tracked caffeine intake. And no space anywhere for drift, for mistake, for misdirection. No space for the part of creativity that *is* uncertainty, the part that doesn't obey efficiency.

I asked him when he last made something without measuring it.

He paused. "College," he said. "Before all this."

So, we dismantled the system. Not all at once. Just in pieces. We took away the dashboard. Let the to-do list breathe. We added unstructured time. Permitted him not to produce anything measurable for a while. It wasn't easy. He twitched for a week. But slowly, something came back. Not just ideas, impulse. Play. Curiosity. The desire to *explore* rather than execute.

That's what optimization can strip from us if we're not careful. The space between intention and outcome. The wiggle room where real learning happens.

It's not just creatives who feel this. It's everyone—parents who measure their children's development against milestones instead of memories. Teachers are pressured to quantify learning instead of cultivating wonder. Entrepreneurs who can't enjoy success because they're too busy scaling. Even rest becomes something to optimize. "How efficiently can I relax?" we ask, and overlook the absurdity.

What we lose in this obsession with refining ourselves is the ability to improvise. To respond. To be surprised. Uncertainty isn't a flaw in the system; it *is* the system. The parts we call noise are often where the truth is hiding.

I've had to retrain myself to tolerate the mess. To work without overdesigning the process. To write without knowing the ending. To rest without tracking how restorative it was. It feels rebellious at first, like you're slacking. But eventually you realize: this isn't slacking. This is a return to the natural unpredictability of being alive.

When optimization is taken too far, it narrows our tolerance for uncertainty and makes us resistant to anything that can't be neatly controlled or measured. Yet, many of the most important aspects of life, love, grief, intuition, creativity, and courage defy such control and measurement, making this resistance a significant limitation. Because of this, I've begun to design my systems with a different approach. I now ask myself whether a given tool or routine increases my adaptability or reinforces rigidity. I consider whether it helps me engage more deeply with uncertainty or allows me to avoid it. I reflect on whether the habits I build serve my core values or feed my anxiety. Above all, I question whether these choices are making me more fully human or turning me into a machine. Sometimes the answers are obvious; often, they are not. But asking these questions helps me avoid drifting too far into the illusion that life can be perfectly engineered.

There's a paradox here, of course. I'm writing these chapters in a structured way. I'm outlining, pacing, and revising. But I'm also leaving room for intuition. I'm not trying to optimize every sentence. I'm trying to let the work breathe. Because if I don't, the soul goes missing. And no level of polish can fix that.

We are not meant to be optimized. We are meant to be alive. And aliveness includes uncertainty, not as an obstacle, but as a condition.

So let the data help you, but don't let it define you. Let the systems support you, but don't let them sedate you. And when the desire to optimize starts to feel like a religion, step back and remember that some of the most important things you will ever feel, do, or become cannot be planned, tracked, or scaled.

They can only be lived.

# Chapter 7: Why Risk Feels Personal

We like to think of risk as a technical concept, percentages, probabilities, and forecasts—something we can calculate, categorize, and mitigate. But when you're the one making the call, when the decision could change your future, ruin your finances, strain your relationships, or challenge your identity, risk doesn't feel mathematical. It feels emotional. It feels like standing on the edge of something with no railing.

The first time I felt real risk wasn't when I started my business, or when I left a job, or even when I poured savings into a project. It was when I told the truth in a room full of people I respected. Not a scandal, just a conviction, something I believed that went against the grain. And as I said it out loud, my heart pounded the way it does when you sense you're about to be exiled. Because at its core, risk isn't about the outcome. It's about the loss you imagine if things go wrong. And more often than not, that loss isn't money or time, it's identity.

When we talk about "taking risks," we usually mean "doing something that could lead to failure." But failure isn't always what we fear. What we fear is what that failure might *tell* about us, that we're not smart. That we're not competent. That we're not lovable, not credible, not enough. We fear the judgment that might follow, the narrative that might form, the shame that might stick. Therefore, we avoid the risk not because it's big, but because it's *personal*.

I've seen this up close in people who've spent years not making a move they know they need to make. The woman who stays in a corporate job she hates because being the breadwinner is her whole identity. The artist who keeps tweaking the same piece for years, terrified to release it because once it's out, it can be judged. The entrepreneur who refuses to launch until the model is airtight, not because he's a perfectionist, but because deep down, he believes one failed launch will confirm every doubt he's ever had about himself.

We think of risk as situational. But it's deeply autobiographical.

It's shaped by our history, our upbringing, our traumas, and the way we were praised or punished. It's shaped by the stories we've absorbed about what's safe, what's smart, what's admirable. If you grew up in a house where mistakes were punished, your threshold for risk is going to be lower, even if you're brilliant. If you were taught that love is conditional on performance, risk will always carry the threat of abandonment, no matter how rational you try to be.

This is why two people can look at the same decision and feel completely different about it. One sees opportunity. The other considers exposure. One sees a possibility. The other sees danger. The variables are the same, but their meanings differ. Because risk isn't just about what might happen, it's about what it might *prove.*

For a long time, I thought I had a high tolerance for risk. I took big swings. I changed careers. I bet on ideas. But when I looked closer, I realized I was only comfortable with certain kinds of risk, mainly the ones where I could still control the narrative. I wasn't afraid to fail *in private.* I was terrified of failing *in public.* Scared that if people saw me stumble, they would revise their opinion of me. And that revision, in my mind, felt like a kind of death. I curated my risks. I made sure that even my bold moves looked polished. I disguised hesitation as strategy. I dressed fear in the language of prudence.

It worked, for a while. But it was exhausting. Because underneath every move was a secret calculation: how do I keep growing without ever being seen failing? And the answer is, you don't.

Eventually, I had to confront the more profound truth: my fear wasn't about the risks themselves. It was about what I believed they would say about *me*. That was the poison. That was the thread running through every moment of hesitation. And naming it, out loud, without flinching, was the beginning of something freer.

I've come to believe that the most honest risk assessment starts not with the spreadsheet, but with the mirror. Before you ask, "What might I lose?" ask, "What story am I trying to protect?" What identity, what status, what illusion? Because often, what makes a decision hard isn't the risk itself, it's the cost to the person we've convinced ourselves we need to be.

There's a story I come back to often. A friend of mine was on the verge of leaving his job to start a nonprofit. He'd done the homework, raised the money, and built the partnerships. But he couldn't pull the trigger. Not because the plan was flawed, but because the image of himself as a "respectable executive" was so tightly woven into his self-worth. "What if it doesn't work?" he asked me. "What if I go from someone people admire to someone they pity?"

I didn't have an answer. But I knew the question was the real risk, not the business plan, not the financials, but the identity shift—the fear of becoming someone he didn't recognize. The fear of watching his old life disappear and not knowing what would grow in its place.

That's why risk always feels bigger than it looks on paper. Because we're not just betting on outcomes, we're betting on versions of ourselves. And that's what makes uncertainty difficult to live with. Not because it's dangerous, but because it destabilizes the narrative. It threatens to unravel the story we've spent years curating.

But maybe that's the point.

Maybe the role of risk isn't just to shake things up externally, but to invite us into a more honest relationship with who we are. Perhaps the fear isn't a signal to stop, but a clue that we're nearing the edge of something important. Something that isn't just tactical, but transformational.

That doesn't mean every risk is worth taking. Some risks are reckless. Some are poorly timed. Some carry consequences that aren't ours alone to bear. But there's a difference between discernment and avoidance. Between caution and paralysis. Between prudence and self-protection disguised as logic.

The only way I've learned to tell the difference is to check where the fear is coming from. Is it fear of loss? Or fear of exposure? Is it the voice of wisdom, or the echo of shame? Is it a gut instinct saying, "not now," or a trauma pattern saying "never"?

These are not quick questions. They take time. And courage. And sometimes, conversation. But asking them has changed the way I move through risk. I don't try to erase the fear anymore. I try to decode it.

Because once you understand why the risk feels personal, it stops controlling you. It still matters, but it no longer dictates. You get to choose what to carry forward and what to lay down.

And here's the other thing I've learned: risk has a twin.

Opportunity.

They're not separate. They're two faces of the same coin. You don't get one without the other. You don't get to grow without exposure. You don't get to lead without vulnerability. You don't get to love without uncertainty. The more alive the decision, the more risk it will carry. That's not a flaw in the design; it *is* the design.

So now, when something feels risky, I try not to run. I try to look closer. I try to ask what part of me is being challenged, not to be erased, but to be evolved.

Because that's what risk can do if you let it; it doesn't just change your circumstances. It changes *you.* It forces a confrontation with your edges. And if you're brave enough to stay in that discomfort, long enough, honestly enough, you'll find something more stable than safety.

You'll find self-trust.

Not the kind that says, "I know I'll succeed," but the kind that says, "Even if I fail, I'll still be me. And that will be enough."

# Chapter 8: The Comfort of Predictable Lies

There's a strange relief that comes with a lie you already know. It doesn't challenge you. It doesn't force you to reconsider anything. It lets you nod along and get on with your day. It may not be true, but it's stable. It has a shape. It has rhythm. And in a world that keeps shifting underfoot, predictability can start to feel like truth, even when you know better.

I've believed a few of those lies. Not because I was naive, but because I was tired. Tired of ambiguity. Tired of second-guessing. Tired of the psychic weight of not knowing. And so, like most people, I grabbed onto something that *sounded* right, something neat, something digestible. Something that let me delay the more complex questions.

Here are a few of the greatest hits:

**"Hard work always pays off."**
**"If you follow your passion, success will follow."**
**"Good things come to those who wait."**
**"Everything happens for a reason."**
**"You're either growing or dying."**

These phrases sound profound in isolation. They're catchy, clean, self-contained. But when I've tested them against real life, they collapse under their weight. Hard work pays off, until it doesn't. Passion is a compass, until it's a trap. Waiting sometimes brings rewards, and sometimes leaves you waiting. And as for growth, I've seen people thrive not because they kept growing, but because they stopped chasing artificial expansion.

But still, I've repeated these lies. I've taught them. I've shared them in presentations, articles, and conversations with people seeking advice. Not because I believed them entirely, but because I didn't know what else to offer. I thought that giving someone a solid-sounding answer was better than leaving them with silence.

Now I'm not so sure.

Predictable lies are dangerous not because they're false, but because they're easy. They offer the illusion of clarity without the burden of investigation. They give us a map that *looks* like the terrain, even if it leads us in circles. And once we're inside that map, it becomes harder and harder to admit we're lost, because to admit we're lost would mean questioning not just the story, but the person we became while believing it.

That's the stickiest part. The lies we cling to are rarely about facts. They're about identity. They tell us who we are, what we deserve, and how the world is supposed to work. Let go of the lie, and the scaffolding starts to wobble.

I worked with someone once, a competent, talented consultant, who built her whole career around the story that being the most prepared person in the room guaranteed respect. It had worked for years. But then a younger, louder, less competent colleague leapfrogged her in the org chart. And suddenly her map didn't make sense anymore. The lie had been comfortable. But reality was indifferent to the rules she'd internalized. Her confusion wasn't just strategic. It was existential. She wasn't just asking, "How do I adapt?" She was asking, "Who am I if this isn't true?"

I see this in organizations, too. The myth of meritocracy. The fantasy of culture fit. The belief that data is neutral. These are stories told not to illuminate, but to smooth over tension. They reduce uncertainty by pretending it isn't there. They allow people to move without scrutinizing what guides them.

Even in relationships, we do this. "They'll change." "It's just a phase." "Love is enough." We repeat these phrases not because they're accurate, but because they buy us time. Because the truth, that things are unstable, or unequal, or broken, is too overwhelming to face without a plan. And when you don't have a plan, sometimes a good-sounding lie is all you've got.

But here's what I've learned: predictable lies always come with a cost. They anesthetize the part of you that wants to see clearly. They dull your instincts. They erode your capacity to respond to what's happening. And the longer you believe them, the more investment you accumulate, the harder it becomes to backtrack without tearing something valuable down.

I've had to unlearn many stories that once made me feel safe. Stories about how success works. About how relationships work. About how identity works. Some of these untruths weren't taught to me maliciously; they were inherited, passed down like family recipes. But once I started living outside their logic, they began to taste wrong.

And then there are the lies I told myself.

That I was fine. That I didn't need help. That I had it figured out. These weren't grand delusions. Just small, consistent reassurances I whispered to avoid facing discomfort. They kept me moving and productive. But they also kept me disconnected from parts of myself that were asking for attention.

What's tricky is that some lies look productive on the outside. They generate results. They help you meet deadlines, hit goals, and get applause. But the result isn't the whole story. If the process requires you to gaslight yourself, if it demands that you ignore your uncertainty, silence your intuition, or pretend your fears don't exist, then you're not succeeding. You're surviving under duress.

There's a reason we prefer predictable lies to unpredictable truths. Because truth often feels incomplete. It rarely comes with a satisfying resolution. It requires interpretation, curiosity, and context. And worst of all, it changes. What's true for you now might not be true in six months. And that kind of fluidity is profoundly threatening to a culture obsessed with final answers.

But maybe the point isn't to find final answers.

Maybe the point is to get better at *staying with the question.*

Maybe truth, especially in uncertain times, is less about what we *know* and more about what we're willing to *notice—noticing* what's real, even when it contradicts our story and seeing what hurts, even when we're expected to smile. Noticing what no longer fits, even when it worked before.

This kind of truth doesn't come from slogans. It comes from attention. From the quiet, repetitive work of asking, "What's happening here?" and resisting the urge to reach for something cleaner.

I don't always get this right. I still reach for straightforward explanations when I'm tired or overwhelmed. I still catch myself trying to tidy up the mess so I can move on. But I've built a few internal alarms over the years. Little signals that tell me when I'm veering into the realm of the comfortable lie. A tightening in the chest. A vague sense of disconnection. A quiet voice that says, "That sounds good, but is it real?"

And when I hear it, I try to stop. I try to sit still. I try to feel the full weight of whatever is unresolved. It doesn't always bring clarity right away. Sometimes it just brings more questions. But that's okay because clarity earned is stronger than certainty handed down.

The older I get, the more I believe that wisdom isn't about knowing more. It's about needing fewer lies. It's about being able to sit with uncertainty without flinching. About learning to live without scaffolding made of stories you no longer believe.

That doesn't mean you abandon structure. It means you build it with your eyes open. Knowing it's provisional. Knowing it might change and knowing that what feels true now is only ever the next iteration of attention.

The world is not tidy. Our lives are not formulas. And meaning is not always efficient.

But if we can learn to tolerate the silence between the lies, if we can resist the urge to fill it with something smooth, we might start to hear something real. Something unpolished. Something true enough to stand on, even if only for a moment.

And maybe, in the end, that's enough.

# Chapter 9: Catastrophizing, Avoidance, and Other Modern Rituals

It starts with a flicker. A piece of news. A text that lands sideways. A look on someone's face that you can't quite read. And before you know it, your mind is galloping ahead to every worst-case scenario it can conjure. You're bankrupt. You're sick. You're alone. You've said something unforgivable, made a mistake you didn't notice, missed a sign that should have been obvious. Your brain isn't analyzing anymore, it's scripting disaster. And even as the rational part of you whispers that you're spiraling, the rest of you is already packing for the apocalypse.

Catastrophizing is something I've done for as long as I can remember. I used to think of it as a flaw. Now I see it as a ritual. A modern form of self-protection dressed in the clothes of imagination. In a world where uncertainty feels ambient and endless, imagining the worst can feel like a form of control. If I can predict the disaster, maybe I can prevent it. If I can suffer it in advance, perhaps it won't hurt so much when it arrives.

But of course, that's not how it works. Anticipated pain doesn't inoculate us against actual pain. It just means we suffer twice, once in the fantasy and once in the moment. Or worse, we suffer endlessly in anticipation of a moment that never even comes.

I've caught myself doing this on quiet mornings. Nothing is wrong. The coffee is hot. The inbox is calm. And then I check the news. Or reread an email. Or think about a project that's not quite resolved. And my brain, eager to feel useful, starts running simulations. Not the good kind. Not creative visualizations or healthy contingencies. I mean doom scenarios—the kind where everything falls apart and it's all somehow my fault.

What's strange is how *familiar* that state can feel. Almost comforting in its way. There's a rhythm to anxiety. A predictability to spiraling. It gives your mind something to do. It spares you from the discomfort of sitting with a world that doesn't offer closure.

And that, I think, is the heart of it. Catastrophizing isn't just a fear response; it's a way to escape ambiguity. To turn the fog of the unknown into the clarity of dread. It transforms the unbearable tension of *maybe* into the painful certainty of *definitely bad.* Which, as backward as it sounds, can feel like relief.

Avoidance works the same way.

Where catastrophizing is hyperactive fear, avoidance is quiet fear. It's the pause that stretches too long. The draft that stays unsent. The phone call you plan to make once things "settle down." It's the email you don't open, the symptom you ignore, the decision you keep moving to next week's to-do list.

Avoidance wears many masks: busyness, perfectionism, and prioritization. But underneath, it's almost always about not wanting to face something that might be bigger than your capacity to control it. A feeling. A truth. A loss. A change.

I've delayed many things under the banner of being "strategic." I've called it timing. I've called it wisdom. But if I'm honest, most of the time I was just scared. Scared that opening that box, literal or emotional, would unleash something I didn't know how to manage. I waited. And waited. And built rituals around the waiting.

That's what these behaviors become over time: rituals. Not choices, not tactics. Patterns so ingrained they stop feeling like decisions at all. You don't *decide* to catastrophize. You don't *choose* to avoid. It's reflexive. You get a twinge of uncertainty, and the ritual begins. The mind lights up with threat-detection. The body tightens. The focus narrows. You start scanning for danger, and if you don't find any, your brain gets creative and manufactures some.

We like to think of ourselves as rational actors, but we are mostly just clever animals trying to reduce perceived threat. In a less connected, slower world, that meant checking the perimeter and sleeping lightly. In this world, it means a refreshing email. Over-researching. Compulsively checking our health, our relevance, our social standing. It means reading three articles on a topic we're already qualified to decide on, just in case we missed something. It means ghosting people we care about because we don't know how to have the conversation.

Avoidance and catastrophizing may look different on the surface, but they serve the same purpose: they let us feel like we're doing *something* in the face of what we can't control.

And they are exhausting.

Because underneath them is a constant vigilance. A belief that if you ever let your guard down, the thing you've been trying to outrun will finally catch up. You keep moving. Keep scanning. Keep managing. But no matter how far you run, you're still carrying the fear with you. And eventually, the rituals stop working. You burn out. You go numb. You make a mistake from fatigue, and suddenly, the thing you were trying to prevent becomes more likely *because* of how hard you were trying to avoid it.

I've seen this in myself. I've seen it in clients. I've seen it in people I love.

And I don't have a fix.

What I do have is a different way of looking at it.

Instead of trying to stop the rituals, I've started treating them as signals. When I notice myself spiraling into disaster fantasy, I try to ask: What am I terrified of? What need is going unmet? Is it safe? Is it clarity? Is it validation? And what might happen if I stayed in the discomfort a little longer instead of trying to resolve it with panic?

When I catch myself avoiding something, I try to name the cost of not facing it. Not in the abstract, but concretely. What relationship is being strained by this silence? What opportunity is being delayed by this hesitation? What version of myself am I keeping at bay by refusing to move?

And most importantly, I try to remember that neither of these rituals, catastrophizing or avoidance, is a sign of weakness. They are adaptations. They were built to help me survive. They don't help me *live*.

Living requires engagement. Presence. The ability to sit with "I don't know" and not immediately replace it with "it's probably terrible." It requires learning to breathe through the ambiguity instead of sprinting toward false clarity. It requires opening the email, making the call, showing up messy and unsure, and being human.

There's no badge for this kind of work. No metric. No applause. Just a quiet shift in how it feels to move through the day. Less tension. More space. A slightly looser grip on the steering wheel.

That's what I aim for now, not certainty, not invincibility, but flexibility. The ability to move without panicking. To pause without freezing. To act without overcontrolling.

Some days I manage it. Some days I don't. But the ritual is shifting. And that, I think, is the real work, not eliminating the fear, but retraining the ritual.

Because in the end, we're all just trying to make sense of a world that doesn't come with guarantees. And while it may be tempting to retreat into the old grooves, to rewatch our favorite disasters in the mind's theater, there's something braver, and far more honest, about staying in the unknown a little longer.

Not because it's easy. But because it's real.

# Chapter 10: Losing the Script

There's a moment, if you live long enough, when the script no longer fits. The lines you've been reciting, about who you are, what success looks like, how life is supposed to unfold, start to sound hollow. You try to deliver them with conviction, the way you always have, but something is off. It's like being in a play where the lighting has changed and the set has moved, but no one told you. You're still acting. But the scene has shifted. And somewhere deep down, you know: it's time to let go of the script.

I've lived through that moment more than once. The first time was subtle. I had followed all the right cues: education, ambition, and opportunity. I hit my milestones like clockwork. But when I looked around, nothing felt earned. It felt staged. The goals weren't mine. The rhythm wasn't mine. I was performing a version of success I no longer believed in. And that realization was terrifying.

Because the script gives you cover, it gives you direction. It tells you where to stand and what to say next. It's the comfort of structure, even if the content is stale. And walking off-script doesn't just feel like rebellion. It feels like annihilation. Who are you if you're no longer playing the role you rehearsed?

That's the question that hits hardest. Not "What should I do now?" but "Who am I without this?" Without the plan, the title, the path. Without the identity you spent years building so carefully, so publicly. When that identity cracks, when the scaffolding starts to fall, it doesn't matter how self-aware you think you are. It feels like freefall.

I've seen this in others, too. The executive who steps down and doesn't know how to introduce herself at dinner parties. The parent whose child leaves home and who suddenly feels unmoored. The athlete whose body changes faster than their self-concept can adapt. In each case, the outer role fades, and what's left is the rawness of uncertainty. The person behind the persona. The actor with no lines.

Most of us resist that moment as long as we can. We try to rewrite the old script instead of letting it go. We look for upgraded versions of the same story. We say we're "pivoting" or "evolving" when we're trying to salvage the identity that's slipping through our fingers. We edit. We rebrand. We double down.

But there comes a point when the rewrite won't work, when the bones of the story are too brittle. When continuing to play the part costs more than walking offstage. And that's when the real work begins, not of finding the following script, but of learning to live without one for a while.

It's disorienting. Scripts are linear. Life without one is anything but. You wake up and don't know what to aim at. You second-guess your instincts. You mourn the clarity you once had, even if it was false. And the people around you, well-meaning as they are, don't always understand. They want to help you "figure it out." They want to see you land somewhere. They want you to make sense again.

But that pressure to make sense is what keeps many people stuck in stories they've outgrown. We impose coherence where none exists. We shape our choices to match expectations. We contort ourselves to appear consistent, even when consistency is killing us.

I remember telling a friend, during one of those liminal stretches, "I don't know who I am anymore." And instead of rushing to reassure me, she said, "Good." She smiled and added, "It means you're getting closer." That phrase lodged itself somewhere deep. Closer to what? I wasn't sure. But something about her response permitted me to stop panicking.

What I was experiencing wasn't a collapse. It was shedding. I wasn't losing myself. I was losing a version of myself that had served its purpose. The script had gotten me here. It had helped me build, connect, and perform. But now it was keeping me from hearing what the moment was asking for.

And that's the paradox. We need scripts, especially early on. They give us direction when we're still building our compass. They provide us with language when we're still finding our voice. But at some point, they become cages. We mistake fluency for truth. We confuse momentum with alignment. And we forget that just because we're moving doesn't mean we're becoming.

Letting go of the script isn't a rejection of everything that came before. It's an act of honesty. A willingness to say, "This is no longer true for me." Not because it never was, but because we've changed. And the world has changed. And what fits once doesn't fit now.

This moment of unscriptedness is not clean. It's awkward. You stumble. You say the wrong thing. You question your motives. You feel exposed. But you also start to feel something else: presence. You begin noticing details again. You start asking real questions. Not "What's next?" but "What's real?" Not "How do I win?" but "What feels right?" Not "What do they expect?" but "What do I know, quietly, in my bones?"

And slowly, if you let that silence speak, something else begins to form. Not a new script. A new way of listening. A new relationship to uncertainty. You no longer need the spotlight to know you're doing something worthwhile. You stop measuring your life in applause. You start making choices from a place that isn't about strategy; it's about alignment.

That kind of living is quieter. It's less glamorous. It doesn't always translate on social media. But it's sustainable. Because it's sourced from inside, and once you've lived that way, even briefly, you can't go back. The old scripts start to itch. The old roles begin to feel like costumes. And the idea of pretending, even if it's lucrative, even if it's admired, becomes intolerable.

This isn't a call to burn it all down. It's a call to check the lines you're still reciting. Ask yourself whose story you're telling. Ask where the plot is heading. Ask who benefits from your performance, and who gets silenced. Ask what would happen if you stepped offstage for a while, not to disappear, but to re-enter your life without the mask.

That takes courage. It's easier to keep performing. Especially when the role has fans. But here's what I know: nothing costs more than playing a part that no longer fits.

Eventually, the audience leaves. The curtain drops. And you're left with the question that outlasts every performance: not "Was it impressive?" but "Was it mine?"

# Chapter 11: Emotional Weather and Internal Forecasts

I've always envied people who seem to wake up the same way every day, steady, neutral, predictable. Like emotional weathervanes always pointing due north. I am not one of those people. My mornings start like forecasts in flux. Some days I rise into stillness. Other days, I'm already inside a storm, unseen by the world, but loud inside my head. And for years, I treated this internal volatility like a flaw. Like evidence that I wasn't calibrated enough, evolved enough, professional enough. But now I know: this emotional weather is not a problem to be fixed. It's a pattern to be read.

What's difficult is that most of us were never taught how to read it. We were taught to suppress it, push through it, or ignore it entirely. Emotional noise is inconvenient. It slows down meetings. It complicates negotiations. It challenges logic. And in a culture obsessed with optimization and certainty, anything that can't be explained in numbers or packaged in tidy language is suspect.

So we develop rituals for pretending we feel fine. We take our bad mood into our inbox and write polite emails. We take our dread into our relationships and call it a distraction. We try to quarantine our internal weather from our external behavior. Sometimes we succeed. But that separation comes at a cost, usually our ability to trust our signals.

Because emotions *are* signals. Not flawless ones, but important ones. They carry information that doesn't always show up in a spreadsheet. That gut feeling before a bad deal? That tightening in your chest before saying yes to something you should decline? Those aren't just moods. They're forecasts— indicators of pressure systems forming below the surface.

The trouble is, we often don't wait long enough to read the pattern. We label the emotions —such as anxiety, fatigue, and restlessness —and then immediately try to fix them. We reach for distraction. We double down on discipline. We tell ourselves it's just a phase, just a glitch in the system—anything to avoid admitting that the feeling might be trying to tell us something.

I used to treat my internal weather like background noise. Something to manage while I got on with the real work. If I felt unmotivated, I'd overschedule myself. If I felt anxious, I'd add structure. If I felt sad, I'd drown it in productivity. The result was that I looked extremely functional, but I wasn't listening to myself at all. I was silencing my radar.

It wasn't until a tough year, one marked by illness, loss, and professional stagnation, that I started paying closer attention. My emotions weren't just louder. They were more complex. Harder to flatten into neat categories. I'd wake up with dread, assuming it was about money, only to realize later that it was about disconnection. I'd feel irritable during meetings, only to discover I was mourning something I hadn't named yet.

At first, I tried to fix it like always. More structure. More calls. More goals. But the patterns didn't change. They deepened. And eventually, I was forced to sit down, not with a plan, but with the weather inside me. I started asking different questions: What's the shape of this feeling? Where does it live in my body? What memories does it stir? What is it asking me to notice?

Those questions didn't provide answers. But they did something more valuable: they made me a better forecaster of my internal climate.

Because that's what most of us need, not emotional neutrality, but emotional fluency. The ability to detect a low-pressure system before it becomes a crisis. The ability to recognize joy without demanding it justifies itself—the ability to name sorrow without having to apologize.

I've come to think of this as developing an "emotional barometer", a capacity to sense, describe, and respect your internal shifts. Not so you can control them, but so you can navigate them. Like any weather system, emotions are not fixed. They roll in. They build. They recede. The goal isn't to eliminate the rain. It's to carry an umbrella and stop pretending it's sunny when it isn't.

This matters not just for personal well-being, but for decision-making. I've made some of my worst calls when I was emotionally disoriented and refused to admit it—said yes to things out of guilt—declined opportunities out of misplaced fear—initiated change out of boredom masquerading as insight. And every time, the root cause wasn't poor logic; it was poor listening. I was misreading the forecast or ignoring it altogether.

But when I do pause, when I give myself a moment to ask "What's happening inside me right now?" something softens. The panic reduces. The compulsive need to *do something* quiets down. And from that quieter place, better questions emerge. Questions not shaped by fear, but by curiosity.

The hardest part of this work is that it doesn't produce immediate results. There's no dashboard. No real-time metric to track your internal literacy. It feels slow. Sometimes indulgent. But over time, it builds something essential: self-trust. Not the kind that says, "I always know what to do," but the kind that says, "I'm paying attention, even when I don't have an answer yet."

That kind of trust is rare, especially in environments that reward speed over reflection. But it's the foundation of resilience. Because when the external world gets chaotic, and it will, your ability to forecast your internal state becomes the anchor. You can't control the market. You can't control how people respond to you. But you can learn to detect when your system is veering off-course.

You can notice when your enthusiasm is anxiety dressed up in ambition.

You can catch when your optimism is a mask for avoidance.

You can name the grief underneath your anger.

And in doing so, you give yourself the dignity of context. You become less reactive, not because you've numbed yourself, but because you're better calibrated. Less likely to confuse a passing storm for a permanent climate. Less likely to flee a discomfort that's trying to teach you something.

I wish this were taught more widely. I want schools, workplaces, and families to have a language for emotional weather. Imagine how much less conflict we'd have if people could say, "I'm in a low-pressure system today. I might need more time, or less noise." Imagine how different leadership would look if it included forecasting as a skill, not just market trends, but human moods, internal dynamics, and unspoken fears.

We've been trained to see emotion as a liability. But what if it's an intelligence? Not a logic replacement, but a complement.

Not a weakness, but a kind of radar. One that doesn't always speak in sentences, but always has something to say.

So now, I check the weather more often. Not just outside, but inside. Before I plan the day. Before I respond to the conflict. Before I make big moves. I ask: What's the forecast today? What's moving in me? What's shifting? What am I pretending not to feel?

Sometimes the answers are fuzzy. Sometimes they're too loud to ignore. But either way, I listen. Not to control the outcome, but to walk more honestly through whatever comes next.

# Chapter 12: Thinking in Probabilities, Not Predictions

I used to think that being smart meant being right. The more accurate your predictions, the more insightful you were. I believed in forecasting as a mark of mastery; if you knew what was coming next, you were prepared, and if you didn't, you weren't. But real life broke that theory over and over again. Not because I stopped learning, but because I finally understood: the world is too complex to predict with certainty. And trying to do so isn't intelligence, it's hubris.

What I've come to believe instead is that intelligent people don't think in predictions. They think in probabilities.

Probabilities don't promise. They estimate. They leave room for doubt, for movement, for surprise. They aren't about certainty; they're about range. And once I made that shift, not just conceptually, but emotionally, my relationship to decision-making changed.

It started when I found myself stuck in a loop of indecision over a business opportunity. On paper, it looked promising: a new revenue stream, an aligned audience, and respected collaborators. But something felt... off. I kept stalling. Not because I had a better option, but because I couldn't guarantee the outcome. I was waiting for the future to clarify itself.

That's what we do when we're addicted to predictions. We pause life, hoping clarity will descend from the sky. We look for signs. We read more books. We poll more people. We run simulations in our heads until our mental battery runs out. All because we want to know for sure.

But here's the secret no one tells you: there is no "for sure." There is only a likelihood. Risk tolerance. Confidence intervals. No decision is ever made with perfect information. We're all just placing bets, every day, on what seems most reasonable given what we know, and then living with what we didn't.

The people who thrive under uncertainty aren't the ones with better answers. They're the ones who accept the structure of reality. They know the game isn't about being right. It's about being approximately correct, often enough, to keep playing.

Once I saw this clearly, I started shifting my questions. Instead of "What's going to happen?" I began asking, "What's likely to happen?" "What's the range of outcomes?" "What's the cost of being wrong?" "How reversible is this if it goes sideways?"

These questions pulled me out of paralysis. They didn't eliminate risk, but they gave it shape. And when risk has shape, it's less scary. You can walk around it. You can decide if it's worth it. You can see where it ends.

Thinking in probabilities isn't natural for most of us. We're wired for stories, for clean cause and effect. We want heroes and villains, breakthroughs and disasters. We don't wish for ambiguity; we want resolution. But life rarely gives us resolution on command. And if we pretend otherwise, we get sloppy. We make absolute declarations about things we only partially understand. We mistake confidence for competence. We ignore signs that don't fit the story we've already sold ourselves.

I've seen leaders destroy good companies by over-believing their predictions. I've watched friends sabotage relationships by assuming worst-case outcomes were certain. I've done both myself, in different ways. And almost every time, the error wasn't in the move; it was in the mindset. I was thinking like a prophet when I should have been thinking like a poker player.

That metaphor, poker, not prophecy, has served me well. In poker, you don't win by playing perfect hands. You win by managing odds, understanding patterns, and knowing when to fold. You win by knowing the difference between a good decision and a good outcome. Because sometimes you play it right and still lose. And sometimes you play it wrong and get lucky. The key is not letting either outcome distort your process.

We don't talk enough about that distinction between process and outcome. We assume that good results mean good thinking. But they often don't. You can be reckless and succeed. You can be meticulous and fail. The only thing you can control is how well you reasoned your way through the unknown.

That's what probabilistic thinking demands. A willingness to hold multiple outcomes at once. To say, "I'm 70% confident this will work," and act accordingly, not as if it's guaranteed, but as if it's favored. And to build a buffer for the other 30%. That's not hedging. That's realism.

It's also humility.

Because probabilities force you to admit you could be wrong. And in a world where status is built on certainty, that's a vulnerable thing to do. But I'd rather be susceptible and adaptable than confident and brittle.

The people I respect most professionally are rarely the loudest. They're the ones who speak in gradients. Who say things like "on balance," "it depends," and "likely, but not guaranteed." Not because they're unsure, but because they understand how little can truly be known in advance.

This is not an excuse to avoid action—quite the opposite. Probabilistic thinkers move sooner. They know waiting for certainty is a trap. They act with what they have, knowing they'll adjust as they go. They make smaller bets, test their assumptions, and update their beliefs. They build decision-making systems that allow for error, not just because error is inevitable, but because it's informative.

One of the most valuable questions I've added to my toolkit is: "What would change my mind?" Before I act, I try to define the conditions under which I'd revisit the choice. That way, I don't get locked into post-hoc rationalization. I don't dig in to save face. I create a plan for responding to uncertainty without panic.

This kind of flexibility doesn't make you less decisive. It makes you more resilient. You stop betting your identity on every choice. You no longer need to be right all the time. You start building a track record of good processes, which, over time, leads to better outcomes anyway.

And you start to feel something rare in high-stakes environments: a sense of ease. Not because the stakes go away, but because you're no longer pretending you can control them. You're in a relationship with uncertainty, not at war with it.

Thinking in probabilities is not just a mental shift. It's an emotional one. It means learning to live in the space between 0% and 100%. Between "definitely not" and "definitely yes." That space is murky. But it's where real life happens. It's where real decisions get made.

And over time, if you can stay in that space without rushing to resolve it, something surprising happens: you stop fearing uncertainty. Not because it's gone, but because you've stopped demanding that it leave.

You know the weather will shift. You know your forecasts won't always be correct. But you also know how to adjust. You trust yourself not to have perfect vision, but to navigate with imperfect tools.

That kind of trust isn't flashy. But it's durable.

And in a world this unpredictable, durability is the new intelligence.

## Chapter 13: Holding Two Truths at Once

There was a time when I believed that clarity meant choosing between competing truths. That if I felt conflicted, it meant I hadn't thought deeply enough or felt honestly enough. I treated contradiction like a failure of logic. But the older I get, and the more uncertainty I've had to live through, the more I've come to understand that complexity isn't something to eliminate. It's something to carry. And sometimes, the most mature thing we can do is hold two truths at once, even when they don't resolve into a clean conclusion.

You can be grateful and grieving. You can feel love and resentment in the same breath. You can be wildly successful by external standards and quietly hollow on the inside. These aren't bugs in the system. They're features of being human.

But that kind of nuance doesn't play well in a culture addicted to resolution. We like our stories clean. Heroes or villains. Wins or losses. Right or wrong. We demand clarity before we've earned it, and then we pressure ourselves to maintain it, even when the lived experience gets messier.

I learned this the hard way during a major life transition that looked, from the outside, like pure progress. I had left a role that no longer fit, launched a new venture that aligned more deeply with my values, and moved to a city I had long wanted to live in. The move was intentional. Every box was ticked. And yet, late at night, I felt a quiet ache I didn't know how to name. I missed the routine I had abandoned. I missed the people I'd worked with, even the ones who'd made life harder. I missed the clarity that came from following a structure I now knew I had outgrown.

At first, I resisted those feelings. I told myself I was being weak, ungrateful, and nostalgic. But the more I pushed them away, the more insistent they became. It wasn't until I stopped trying to solve the contradiction that something shifted. I realized that both things could be true. I could mourn what I left behind without regretting that I left it. I could love what I was moving toward without denying what I had lost. Nothing needed to be deleted to make space for the next chapter.

That was a turning point not just in that situation, but in how I started approaching complexity in general. I stopped expecting my emotions to line up neatly. I stopped interrogating myself every time my values bumped into my desires. I started practicing the uncomfortable but honest skill of holding tension, without forcing resolution.

It's not a comfortable practice.

The mind wants closure. It wants to know which voice is right. Which part of you wins? But often, no part wins. They coexist like roommates who don't particularly like each other but agree to share the space.

I've worked with people who have spent decades trying to suppress one half of their internal dialogue. The parent who loves their children but sometimes longs for the freedom they lost. The founder who believes deeply in their mission but hates the person they've become while building it—the partner who feels devotion and disconnection at once.

We don't know what to do with those contradictions. So, we pathologize them. We label them as confusion, disloyalty, and weakness. We often try to resolve them through action, quitting, ending, or escaping, but what we need is not a decision, but a deeper tolerance for duality.

That's not to say there's never a time for decisive moves. But when we act too quickly to eliminate complexity, we often miss the insight inside it. We miss the chance to understand what the tension is trying to reveal.

Because that's what these internal contradictions are, they're information. There are signs that something important is happening. That your internal system is negotiating change. That you are outgrowing something, or integrating something, or waking up to something you hadn't fully faced.

And if you can stay with that discomfort, if you can resist the urge to resolve too quickly, you start to build a different kind of clarity. Not the clarity of simplification, but the clarity of integration.

I've started to think of this as a kind of emotional ambidexterity, the ability to hold joy in one hand and sorrow in the other, without asking one to cancel the other out. It's a subtle skill. It doesn't get much attention. But it might be the most important trait I've developed in adulthood.

It shows up everywhere now.

- ∞ In decision-making, where I can see both the opportunity and the risk, and choose anyway.
- ∞ In relationships, where I can love someone and still hold boundaries.
- ∞ In leadership, I can carry confidence and humility at the same time.
- ∞ In self-reflection, where I can acknowledge progress without erasing what still hurts.

It hasn't made life easier. But it has made it richer.

Because when you permit yourself to feel more than one thing at once, the world becomes more textured. More honest. Less performative. You no longer need to simplify everything for consumption. You start making peace with the gray.

That's the theme of this entire arc: *living in the grey, not* as a compromise, but as a position of strength. It's easy to live in black and white. It's easy to pick a side, craft a narrative, and ignore the dissonance. But easy is not the same as accurate.

And if you've made it this far in the book, it's probably because you're tired of pretending things are simpler than they are.

So, let's name it:

- ∞ You can want change and fear it.
- ∞ You can believe in your work and still feel like a fraud.
- ∞ You can be a good person and still carry shadows.
- ∞ You can know your value and still crave validation.
- ∞ You can forgive someone and still feel the sting.
- ∞ You can be okay and not okay at the same time.

None of these makes you broken. They make you real.

We don't need to fix every contradiction. We need to learn to hold them with care. To stop asking our lives to resolve like a well-structured screenplay. To stop demanding that clarity arrive on our timeline.

Sometimes, understanding comes after the fact. Sometimes it never comes. But peace doesn't require perfect understanding. It requires acceptance. Not resignation, but recognition. The kind of recognition that says: This, too, belongs. Even if it doesn't make sense yet. Even if it never fully will.

One of the practices I've adopted in recent years is naming the contradictions out loud. Especially when I'm stuck, I'll say, "Part of me wants to stay, and part of me wants to leave." Or "I'm proud of this, and I also feel deeply unsettled." Just naming the paradox softens its grip. It reminds me I'm not malfunctioning. I'm just metabolizing something complex.

It also helps the people around me. When I model emotional complexity, it permits others to do the same. Conversations get deeper. Decisions get slower but more thoughtful. Teams become more humane when we stop pretending everyone's on the same page, since most of us are reading different chapters simultaneously.

That's the world I want to live in. One where nuance isn't punished. One where people don't have to flatten themselves to be understood. One where the truth is allowed to be layered, and decisions are made with awareness, not performance.

We won't get there all at once. But we can start here with the small, brave act of not rushing to solve what can only be carried.

Suppose you're holding two truths right now. If your life is full of tension, contradiction, and unresolved emotion, you're not alone. You're not confused. You're right on time.

You're human.

And maybe, for now, that's the only truth that needs to win.

# Chapter 14: Strategic Indecision

There's a kind of panic that sets in when we don't know what to do next. It's not just the discomfort of being uncertain; it's the fear of being seen as indecisive. We've been trained to believe that good decision-makers move fast. That leaders don't hesitate. That clarity is a virtue, and delay is a sign of weakness. So, when we pause, even for a moment, the internal alarms go off. What's wrong with me? Why can't I decide?

I've lived through that panic many times. There were decisions I felt I *should* be able to make quickly, such as where to move, who to partner with, and which project to pursue, but something in me held back. Not out of fear exactly, but something subtler. A quiet hesitation I didn't know how to justify. And instead of honoring that hesitation, I tried to override it. I scheduled calls, made lists, and ran cost-benefit analyses. I told myself I just needed more data.

But more often than not, the data wasn't the issue. I had enough information. What I didn't have was the internal readiness to move. And instead of respecting that, I treated it like a bug to be fixed. I pressured myself to be decisive when what I needed was to be discerning.

That's the distinction I've come to live by: not all indecision is avoidance. Some of it is strategy.

Strategic indecision is the conscious choice to pause, not because you're confused, but because the conditions aren't right. It's the decision *not* to decide yet, not out of paralysis, but out of respect for complexity. It's the maturity to wait for clarity without demanding it arrive on your timeline.

We don't talk much about this waiting. In business, in relationships, in culture at large, there's enormous pressure to appear decisive. You're expected to "have a take." To make the call. To move forward, even if it means course-correcting later. And sure, that works in some cases. But in others, it leads to unnecessary damage.

I've seen leaders rush into partnerships they later regretted because they didn't want to appear indecisive. I've seen founders launch products that weren't ready because they couldn't tolerate another week of uncertainty. I've seen people accept jobs, enter relationships, or commit to projects that felt off, simply because they thought pausing would make them look weak or flaky.

And I've done all of it myself. Every rushed decision I've made from that place, driven by urgency rather than readiness, has come with hidden costs. Not always catastrophic, but cumulative. Time, energy, and emotional capital spent on untangling things that never needed to be tangled in the first place.

What I've learned is that the pressure to appear decisive is often more substantial than the pressure to be right. We'd rather be confidently wrong than visibly uncertain because uncertainty is vulnerable. It leaves you exposed. It invites questions. It demands you tolerate being seen without a plan.

But sometimes, the best move is no move.

Not forever. Not as a way to hide. But as a way to listen. To watch. To let the context evolve because some decisions make themselves if you give them enough space.

I remember a moment a few years ago when I was considering a significant professional change. Everything on the surface said go, logic, timing, and opportunity. But every time I sat with it, something in me went still. Not scared. Just quiet. Like my internal compass had gone dim, I couldn't tell if I was resisting out of fear or if something deeper was at play.

So I did something that felt wildly countercultural: I stopped pushing. I didn't force the call. I didn't announce a decision. I let the ambiguity stretch out. I told the people involved that I was still listening and still considering. That I needed more time, not more data, but more *signal*.

They didn't love it. A few were confused. Some were impatient. But the clarity came, not in a flash, but in fragments. And when I finally did decide, weeks later, I was grounded. There was no drama. No second-guessing. Just the quiet confidence of having waited long enough to *know*.

That kind of patience is hard to justify, especially in fast-moving environments. But I've come to believe that it's one of the most underrated forms of intelligence: knowing when to act, and knowing when to wait.

Strategic indecision doesn't mean dithering. It doesn't mean avoiding hard calls. It means being intentional about *when* you commit. It means learning the rhythms of your discernment. Knowing how long it takes you to metabolize information. Knowing the difference between procrastination and wisdom.

I keep a simple question on a sticky note above my desk. It says: "Am I waiting because I'm scared, or because I'm listening?"

That question has saved me from both impulsivity and inertia.

Because fear disguises itself as strategy all the time, it tells you to wait, but what it means is "don't risk anything." And when

I feel that kind of fear, I try to move anyway. Not recklessly, but with eyes open. I remind myself that risk is part of the deal.

But when I'm listening, when the pause feels grounded rather than evasive, I've learned to trust it. I've learned to let the fog roll in, and instead of driving blind, I pull over. I wait. I pay attention to what emerges in the slowness. Often, it's something I hadn't even considered when I was in execution mode.

The truth is, a lot of life happens in these in-between spaces. The moment after the offer but before the reply. The days between endings and beginnings. The stretch of stillness before the new shape of your life arrives.

We tend to rush those spaces. But they matter. They're not dead zones. They're compost. Fertile ground where the next move starts to take form, not in a flash, but as a slow-growing knowing.

I no longer see indecision as a failure. I see it as a skill in progress. A relationship to time. A discipline of restraint.

And I no longer feel the need to perform clarity I don't yet have. Because the pressure to appear decisive is not the same as the call to act, you can feel both and choose to wait.

You can say, "I'm not ready to decide," and still be accountable. You can say, "I need more time," and still be trustworthy. You can say, "I don't know yet," and still be a leader.

That's the gift of strategic indecision; it gives you back the right to pause, to watch, to gather what can't be rushed.

It teaches you to live inside the question a little longer, until the answer reveals not just itself, but your readiness to hold it.

# Chapter 15: Control vs. Influence

There's a question I've learned to ask myself when things get chaotic, when plans unravel, when people don't behave the way I think they should: Am I trying to control this, or am I trying to influence it?

It sounds simple. But hidden inside that distinction is an entire philosophy of how to move through an unpredictable world.

Most of us grow up equating responsibility with control. If you care about something, you should own it. Manage it. Please keep it on track. And if it veers off course, it must be because you didn't try hard enough. You weren't disciplined enough. You didn't push the right levers. That belief gets internalized early and reinforced constantly. It looks like ownership. It seems like ambition. But often, it's just anxiety wearing a suit.

I've spent most of my adult life navigating between these two mindsets, striving to be someone who takes initiative without becoming someone who tries to control everything. And it's a razor-thin line. The moment you overstep, influence becomes control. Support becomes manipulation. Leadership becomes micromanagement. And your ability to navigate uncertainty vanishes, because now you're fighting the world instead of responding to it.

The illusion of control is comforting. It gives us something to hold. Something to blame. Something to do. When a situation feels unstable, our instinct is to tighten our grip. We call more meetings. We revise the budget again. We check on people who haven't asked to be checked on. We step in, not because it helps, but because it soothes the discomfort of feeling powerless.

But control is brittle. It doesn't scale. It doesn't flex. And the more you rely on it, the more reactive you become. Every deviation feels like a threat. Every delay feels like failure. Every other person becomes a variable to manage instead of a person to engage.

I've had to learn this lesson over and over, especially in relationships and in leadership.

There was a time when I mistook helping for being in charge. If someone was struggling, I stepped in. If a project hit a snag, I tried to fix it myself. I told myself I was being responsible. But really, I was trying to ease my discomfort with other people's ambiguity. I couldn't stand watching someone I cared about go through a process I couldn't predict. I couldn't tolerate loose ends, even when those loose ends weren't mine to tie.

The result? I exhausted myself. I robbed others of their agency. And I carried the false burden of outcomes I never actually controlled.

That's when I started exploring the idea of influence, not as a buzzword, but as a mindset. Influence doesn't seek to dominate. It aims to engage. It asks, What can I offer here that might be useful? What access, perspective, resources, or presence do I have that might change the trajectory of this situation without needing to own the outcome?

∞ Influence respects boundaries. Control ignores them.
∞ Influence works with reality. Control tries to overwrite it.
∞ Influence adapts. Control resists.

The difference shows up in small moments. When someone vents to you about a problem, your immediate response is to solve it. Influence listens, asks, "Do you want support or solutions?" When a team misses a deadline, control and oversight become tighter. Influence asks, "What got in the way, and how can we make it easier next time?" When your child makes a decision you disagree with, control lectures. Influence gets curious.

There's power in influence. But it's quiet. It doesn't announce itself. It doesn't guarantee results. And that's what makes it hard to choose, especially in a culture that worships certainty and control.

I've seen people try to influence while secretly craving control. They use softer language, but their energy betrays them. They're still attached to a specific outcome. They still think of success as "getting their way without looking bossy." But influence isn't just a different tactic, it's a different posture. You have to be okay with things not going your way. You have to let go of the fantasy that if you say it well enough, people will agree with you.

Influence is patient. It plants seeds. It makes offers and lets go. And that letting go is the hardest part. Because it means acknowledging that other people are autonomous and that systems are complex, that outcomes are emergent. It means surrendering the need to be right in favor of being real.

Control can get results in the short term. But it does so at the cost of connection, adaptability, and often, sustainability. Influence is slower. It's less predictable. But over time, it builds something far more powerful: trust.

And trust is what makes resilience possible in an uncertain world. Not trust that everything will go to plan, but trust that we'll respond well when it doesn't.

That's why this chapter belongs here, in the middle of *Living in the Grey*. Because the ability to influence without controlling is a hallmark of people who've made peace with uncertainty, they don't need the world to conform to their will to stay grounded. They don't mistake other people's decisions for their failures. They don't need to manage every variable to feel safe.

They move with intention, not insistence.

They show up, offer value, and accept that not everything is theirs to shape.

This is not a passive stance. It's an active commitment to discernment. To know what's yours and what's not. To understand the difference between leadership and domination. Between collaboration and coercion.

For me, the shift began with language. I started changing the way I framed situations internally. Instead of saying, "How do I fix this?" I'd ask, "Where do I have influence here?" Instead of saying, "What's wrong with them?" I'd ask, "What am I assuming I need from them to feel okay?" Instead of saying, "I need this to happen," I'd say, "I'd like this to happen, and here's how I might support that."

It didn't make me less effective. If anything, I got better results. Because people don't resist influence the way they resist control. Influence invites—control demands. And humans, being what we are, respond better to invitation than to orders, especially under stress.

There's a humility in influence that feels profoundly human. It acknowledges that the world is co-created, that no matter our intelligence or skill, we are not all-powerful. Even our most carefully crafted plans rely on timing, collaboration, and factors beyond our control. When we hold this truth, we begin to ease our grip, stop clutching the wheel so tightly, and open ourselves to greater creativity and connection. We become more willing to embrace solutions that weren't in our original blueprint. When you find yourself struggling to steer something resistant to control, pause and ask: Am I trying to control it, or to influence it? And if you can summon the courage, take a step back, contribute what you can, and allow the rest to unfold as it must.

# Chapter 16: The Paradox of Preparation

There's a quiet kind of safety in preparation. A sense that if you think it through hard enough, plan it well enough, anticipate every angle, you can soften the blow of what's coming, or maybe even prevent it altogether. Preparation gives us the illusion of a buffer between us and the unknown. And to a point, that illusion is useful. It keeps us moving. It provides us with the confidence to step forward. But past a certain threshold, it becomes something else: a trap disguised as discipline.

I've spent much of my life preparing not just for the obvious things, meetings, launches, and interviews, but for every imaginable deviation from the plan. I've been ready for conversations that never happened—drafted responses to emails that never arrived. I've rehearsed explanations, rationalizations, and apologies, just in case. I told myself this was wisdom. Foresight. Maturity. But often, it was fear—a way of armoring myself against uncertainty.

The paradox is this: preparation gives you confidence to act, but too much preparation prevents you from acting at all.

There's a threshold beyond which planning stops being empowering and starts being evasive. I used to cross that line all the time, especially in periods of transition. When something new was on the horizon, a career shift, a personal risk, a significant project, I'd go into what I called "readiness mode." It felt productive. I'd gather data, talk to people, sketch models, and simulate outcomes. I'd research every adjacent concept until the outlines blurred. But if I were honest, I wasn't getting more prepared. I was postponing the moment of exposure.

Because that's what action is: exposure. A moment when the idea becomes real, when the draft becomes public, when the risk becomes irreversible. And if you've anchored your safety in preparation, that leap can feel like stepping off a cliff.

I've come to see that preparation is most useful when it's in the service of engagement, not when it replaces it. And the only way to know where that line is, to know when you've prepared enough, is to start moving. That's the paradox. You can only validate your preparation by taking the very step it's meant to support.

And yet, culturally, we reward over-preparation. We praise those who are "thorough," "strategic," and "always ready." But we don't always ask what that readiness costs. The lost opportunities. The conversations that never happened. The versions of ourselves that stayed hidden, waiting for the perfect moment.

The perfect moment, of course, never comes.

I've watched people prepare for years to make a move they could have made in weeks. Not because they weren't capable, but because they weren't willing to meet the moment without guarantees. They wanted the entire staircase before taking the first step. They wanted every possible variable accounted for. And because life doesn't offer that kind of assurance, they stayed stuck. Safe, but stagnant.

I've done this too. And every time, I've had to learn, again, that life isn't a test you can study your way through. It's a dance. And at some point, you have to stop counting beats and start moving your body.

This doesn't mean you should leap unquestioningly—preparation matters. Thoughtfulness matters. But only if it leads to motion. Only if the map eventually gives way to the terrain.

One of the most liberating shifts in my thinking was moving from "Am I ready?" to "Am I willing?" Because readiness is often a moving target. Willingness is something else entirely. It asks: Am I willing to be seen trying? Am I willing to learn in public? Am I willing to adjust midstream instead of waiting for the perfect route?

That shift has changed the way I launch, the way I lead, the way I love. I no longer need to feel 100% prepared to say yes. I need to be willing to meet what comes next with attention and care.

That kind of preparation, the kind that sharpens your response capacity rather than just your plan, is worth cultivating. It's a different posture. Less about prediction, more about presence. Less about control, more about readiness *to respond*.

I've come to think of this as "dynamic preparation." It's not static. It's not built in a vacuum. It evolves as the situation evolves. It assumes that you will need to revise. That new information will surface. That your first attempt might miss the mark. And that none of this is a problem if you've built flexibility into your system.

I once heard a military strategist say, "Plans are useless, but planning is indispensable." That line stayed with me. Because it captures the paradox perfectly. The value of preparation isn't in the plan itself; it's in the readiness it builds. The way it forces you to think through implications, map priorities, and sharpen instincts is particularly valuable. But once the moment arrives, the plan often dissolves. And what remains is your capacity to respond.

So, when people ask me how to know if they're ready, I say: stop asking if the plan is perfect. Ask if you've built the muscle of engagement. Ask if you know how to listen mid-action. Ask if you're willing to be surprised.

Because that's the real work. Not building a flawless script, but building the presence to improvise when the scene changes.

There's a tenderness in this shift. A humility. It requires you to let go of the fantasy that you can outthink risk, that you can pre-empt pain. If you prepare well enough, life won't catch you off guard.

But it will. It always does.

And that's not a failure. That's the nature of the thing.

The people I admire most aren't the ones who always seem ready. They're the ones who know how to recalibrate. Who steps in before they're entirely comfortable. Those who prepare just enough to begin and then let the learning happen in motion.

They understand that you don't grow by waiting for conditions to align. You grow by showing up, paying attention, and adjusting as you go.

So now, when I feel myself slipping into endless preparation, I pause. I ask: What am I avoiding? What's the cost of not moving? And if I had waited for perfect readiness last time, would it have helped?

The answer is almost always no.

And so, I move. Not recklessly. Not prematurely. But willingly. With enough preparation to orient me, and enough openness to meet whatever I didn't plan for.

That's the paradox.

You prepare so that you're ready *to let go of the preparation.*

# Chapter 17: Making Peace with Not Knowing

There are days I still catch myself pretending I know more than I do. I'll nod in conversation when I'm unsure. I'll write with confidence about topics that still feel unsettled inside me. It's not malicious. It's a reflex. The desire to be seen as capable, credible, and transparent. But beneath that reflex is an old discomfort, the ache of not knowing.

Uncertainty isn't just a mental problem. It's a visceral one. You feel it in your chest, your jaw, your breath. It hums in the background of your thoughts, whispering threats your logic can't quite silence. And so, naturally, we look for relief. Some way to resolve the unease. Some explanation. Some answer. We want the unknown to shrink.

And if we can't make it shrink, we try to control how it makes us look.

I spent years building systems to mask my uncertainty. I framed it as curiosity. I buried it under layers of research. I convinced myself that if I just learned enough, the fear would subside. But it didn't. Because the fear wasn't about knowledge, it was about the feeling of being exposed.

We're told that adulthood is about having answers. That maturity is about being sure. But real adulthood, at least the version I've come to respect, is something quieter. It's the capacity to stand calmly in the fog. To name what you don't know without shame. To live inside the open question, not as a victim of it, but as a conscious participant.

That's not easy, especially in environments that reward certainty. Try saying "I don't know" in a boardroom. Or in a relationship conflict. Or on social media. Watch how quickly people start filling in the silence, projecting, advising, correcting. We're allergic to gaps. We rush to fill them, often with noise that only deepens the confusion.

But what if we didn't rush?

What if we let the gap be there?

What if we made peace, not just intellectually, but somatically, with the fact that not knowing is part of the deal?

That's a more challenging task than it sounds. Because not knowing triggers our oldest fears. The fear of being wrong. The fear of being judged. The fear of being left behind. These aren't academic concerns. They're primal. And unless we learn how to soothe those fears, we'll keep pretending. We'll keep armoring ourselves with answers, even when they don't fit.

The shift for me began in the moments I finally admitted I was lost. Not in a dramatic way, just quietly, internally. When I stopped narrating certainty and just said, "I don't know." At first, those words felt like surrender. But over time, they began to feel like the truth. Not a dead end, but a doorway.

Because when you admit you don't know, you become available to learn. Not in the shallow way we often talk about learning, but in the more profound sense. You become porous. Curious. Humble. You listen more carefully. You stop scanning for confirmation and start noticing what's there.

It's like turning off the noise cancellation and finally hearing the texture of the world.

Not knowing also creates space for others to step in. When I stopped pretending to have the answers, people responded with more generosity than I expected. They didn't see me as incompetent. They saw me as human. And that shifted the dynamic. It turned conversations into collaborations. It allowed wisdom to emerge from the group, not just from the person holding the mic.

I began to notice something else, too. The more comfortable I got with not knowing, the more relaxed my body felt. The tension I used to carry in my shoulders started to melt. The mental looping slowed down. My sleep improved. It was as if the nervous system, too, had been waiting for permission to drop the performance.

That's when I realized: certainty isn't a prerequisite for peace. It's often the obstacle.

Because certainty, especially the manufactured kind, is brittle. It can't adapt. It can't hold nuance. It shatters the moment the world fails to cooperate.

But peace? Peace is pliable. It allows for movement. It doesn't demand perfection. It just asks that you stay with what is, without fleeing into fantasy.

Making peace with not knowing doesn't mean you give up on clarity. It means you no longer need clarity to feel grounded. You trust that the fog will lift when it's ready, or not, and either way, you'll find your way through.

You don't abandon the pursuit of understanding. But you abandon the fantasy that understanding will eliminate doubt.

This practice has changed the way I build, the way I write, and the way I relate. I no longer measure my value by how much I know. I measure it by how well I stay engaged when I don't.

When someone asks me a question I don't know how to answer, I try to say so, not as a deflection, but as an honest place to begin. When I reach the edge of my expertise, I mark it. I don't rush to fill the silence. I let it sit. I trust that something helpful can still happen in that space.

Because not knowing is not the same as ignorance. Ignorance is a refusal to engage. Not knowing is an invitation to inquire.

And inquiry, I've found, is far more potent than conclusion.

We tend to think that answers are the goal. But often, the quality of the question is what determines the depth of the insight. And good questions only emerge when we admit we don't already know.

That's what makes not knowing so fertile. It's where creativity lives, where innovation begins. Where relationships deepen. No one wants to be in connection with someone who always has it figured out. What we want is presence. Attunement. A sense that the other person is here, with us, in the mess.

I practice that now; I stay in the mess..

When a friend is grieving and words fail me, I stop trying to fix it. I say, "I don't have the words, but I'm here." When a project feels uncertain and the path forward is unclear, I acknowledge it honestly: "We're in the fog right now, and that's okay." When the future presents too many possibilities to grasp, I resist the temptation to impose a rigid five-year plan and instead say, "Let's take the next right step and stay attentive." This is what embracing not knowing has taught me, a new kind of courage. Not the courage to conquer, but the courage to remain: to remain open, curious, and in relationship with the mystery without rushing to reduce it to something manageable. Yes, it still scares me at times.

The world demands answers; people seek direction; deadlines approach, and expectations build. But increasingly, I find strength in the pause, in the space between "I used to know" and "I don't know yet." That space is far from empty; it is fertile ground where the next version of your life begins to take shape. If you can stand in that space long enough, with enough honesty, something shifts; the fear doesn't vanish, but it softens and loses its hold. Because you come to understand that you can be uncertain and still move forward, incomplete and yet whole, lost in the fog but still able to find your way. You don't have to know everything. You only need to remain awake.

## Chapter 18: Risk, Loss, and the Fragile Win

Every meaningful action I've ever taken has carried with it a whisper of risk. Sometimes it was faint, just a flicker of discomfort, a background hum. Other times, it was deafening. But it was always there. Risk is the shadow companion of any step that matters. And if you're paying attention, it never really goes away. It just changes shape.

The trouble is, we rarely talk about it honestly. We talk about courage. We talk about boldness. We talk about wins. But we don't linger long in the middle, where risk lives. We sanitize the journey for the sake of a clean narrative, as if success were a straight line, as if wins were inevitable once you decided to be brave.

They're not.

The truth is that every real shot comes with the possibility of failure, embarrassment, or even heartbreak. And not in the tidy, motivational sense, where the loss becomes a lesson, and you bounce back stronger. No, I mean real loss. The kind that doesn't make sense right away. The kind that lingers in your stomach when you think back on what could've been.

That's the kind of risk most of us don't prepare for, not emotionally, anyway.

I've lost things I cared about. Ideas I believed in that never landed. Projects I poured myself into that fizzled before they found their rhythm. I've trusted people who didn't follow through and taken leaps that ended in silence. And I've come to understand that this isn't a sign that I did something wrong. It's a sign I was playing for stakes that mattered.

What no one tells you, at least not loudly enough, is that even when things go *right*, there's often a cost. That winning doesn't always feel like triumph. That some victories are fragile, and others are lonelier than you expected. That sometimes you do everything right, and it still hurts.

That's not cynicism. That's clarity.

When you stop romanticizing the outcome, you start preparing for reality. You begin to see risk not as a dragon to slay, but as the weather you choose to walk through because the destination is worth it.

This shift didn't happen for me all at once. I resisted it. I wanted clean wins. I wanted to believe that if I did enough emotional work, if I asked the right questions, if I waited until I was fully ready, I could bypass the pain. But you can't out-think risk. You can only build a relationship with it.

I started treating risk like a traveling companion. I gave it a seat. I stopped trying to evict it before taking action. I stopped looking for the version of life where the stakes were lower and started asking what kind of risks I was willing to take. Do not eliminate, *hold*.

There's a difference.

Avoiding risk is often a disguised attempt to prevent loss. And that's where this chapter lives, in the space between risk and loss. Because to understand one, you have to understand the other.

Loss is not always dramatic. Sometimes it's subtle. The loss of an imagined future. The loss of a version of yourself that no longer fits—the loss of innocence, of certainty, of trust. And even when the outcome is technically a "win," that loss can still cut deep.

I remember landing a significant opportunity a few years ago. It was the kind of break I'd been working toward for years. But when it came, I didn't feel victorious. I felt exhausted. I felt disoriented. I felt, strangely, grief. Because to step into that next level meant leaving behind a simpler, earlier version of my work—a version I'd outgrown but still loved.

That's the fragile win. The moment you get what you wanted, you realize it comes with a cost.

No one posts about that part. The bittersweetness. The reconfiguration of identity. The space between celebration and sadness. But it's there. And if you don't expect it, it can undo you. You'll think you're ungrateful. You'll think something's wrong. When really, you're just feeling the full texture of change.

I've stopped chasing wins that promise only elation. I look now for the ones I'm willing to suffer for. The ones I'm eager to carry grief alongside. The ones that don't require me to pretend the risk wasn't real.

Because the more I live, the more I believe this: you don't get to skip the cost. You get to choose what's worth it.

That's what real risk management is. Not minimizing exposure, but clarifying value. Asking: What am I *willing* to risk, not just what am I *comfortable* risking?

Comfort has its place. But when comfort becomes the metric for action, you end up with a life full of side bets. Safe moves. Padded steps. You never quite go all in. You never reasonably feel the rush or the devastation that comes with playing for real.

And that's the tragedy: not the loss itself, but the life that never got close enough to risk losing something.

There's a clarity that only comes from loss. I wish it weren't true. I wish there were another way to sharpen your understanding of what matters. But every major reorientation in my life has followed something falling apart. And not always in dramatic fashion. Sometimes just a quiet fade, a slow realization, a door that never opened.

Those moments broke something open in me. They taught me what I could survive, what I valued. What I was willing to try again for, even knowing it might hurt again.

That's the kind of resilience I trust, not the forced optimism, but the grounded willingness to re-enter the arena with eyes open.

We need more conversations like this. More honesty about what risk feels like, not just in theory, but in the body. The nausea. The breath-holding. The late-night spirals. The way it never entirely leaves, even when things go well.

We also need more space for those who tried but didn't win. Not as cautionary tales, but as fellow travelers. People who dared. People who bet on something meaningful and came up short. Their stories matter. Not just because they show us what can go wrong, but because they show us what it means to live with intention anyway.

Perhaps most importantly, we need to grow comfortable with the fragile nature of success. We must stop viewing wins as permanent or as definitive proof that we are right. Success is fleeting, a snapshot in time, and it doesn't mean we've escaped risk; instead, it means we're still immersed in it, only on a different plane. If you find yourself standing at the brink of something new, feeling the weight of the choice, the pull of uncertainty, and the soft voice of fear, know this: feeling scared doesn't make you weak, hesitating doesn't make you broken, and grieving what may be lost doesn't make you wrong. It means you are awake. If you can hold that awareness, balancing both risk and hope, you may discover that the most profound victories are those you can't fully articulate. The ones that open your heart wide, that demand a real sacrifice, and that remind you deeply, in your very core, that you are truly alive.

# Chapter 19: When to Burn the Map

I've always loved maps. Not just for the way they chart physical space, but for the comfort they offer, lines and edges, legends and scales, the illusion that if you follow the route, you'll get where you're going. Maps promise clarity. They make the world seem knowable, predictable, and containable. And for a long time, I believed that if I could build the correct map of my life, my work, my relationships, I'd avoid unnecessary detours. I'd outmaneuver regret. I'd win at control.

But there comes a moment in every serious pursuit, every creative act, every mission, every life-altering decision, when the map no longer helps. When the territory you're in has shifted underneath your feet. The roads are gone, or wrong, or were never really there to begin with. You're holding a guide to a place that doesn't exist anymore. And if you keep following it, you don't find safety. You find stagnation.

That's when you have to burn the map.

It sounds dramatic. And it is. But sometimes drama is precisely what the moment calls for. Not because you're being reckless, but because you're being honest. The map you built was based on old information. Old values. Old assumptions. It was never meant to guide you forever. And when you reach the edge of its usefulness, holding on becomes a form of self-sabotage.

I learned this the hard way.

I had a plan, a good one, by conventional standards. It was clear, achievable, and linear. Every step accounted for. Every risk is pre-managed. I'd built a life around it, and to the outside world, it looked like it was working. But inside, something was cracking. I was restless. Detached. And not because I didn't appreciate what I had. I did. But I could feel it: I had outgrown the map.

Still, I clung to it.

That map had gotten me here, after all. It had protected me, shaped me, and kept me moving. It was full of all the right moves, according to someone. I kept consulting it, long after it stopped matching the terrain. I ignored the gut signals, the friction, the false starts. I adjusted my reality to align with the path, rather than altering the path to fit my reality.

Eventually, the misalignment became too loud to ignore. Things that used to excite me felt hollow. Projects I'd once killed to land felt like obligations. Conversations turned mechanical. My goals felt borrowed. And when I finally admitted the truth, that I no longer wanted what I thought I wanted, I was left standing with a handful of ashes and no replacement plan.

That's the terrifying part about burning the map: you don't get a new one right away. Sometimes you don't get one at all. You're walking blind and feeling for a signal in the dark. Measuring forward progress not in miles, but in moments of internal clarity.

But here's the part I didn't expect: the longer you walk without a map, the better you get at navigation.

You learn to read the wind. Body. Emotion. You know which signals to trust. Which paths call to you, not because someone said they mattered, but because you feel more *you* when you're on them.

Burning the map isn't about abandoning direction. It's about releasing false certainty.

It's about choosing presence over projection.

Because most of our maps are projections, they're based on what worked for someone else, or what seemed logical a decade ago, or what felt safe when we were still afraid of our agency. They're built from old fears and inherited metrics. And if you never update them or destroy them when necessary, they become cages.

One of the most freeing decisions I ever made was to step away from a high-profile opportunity that, by every logical measure, should have marked a significant milestone. But it wasn't truly mine. It didn't resonate with who I had become. It required a version of myself I had already left behind. Continuing down that road would have meant quietly betraying my integrity over time. I let it go without having a next step lined up, no master plan, no carefully crafted pivot. I deliberately stepped into the unknown. That choice didn't turn me into a hero; it made me scared, broke, confused, and, for a while, without direction. Yet, it also brought me back to authenticity and, in time, led me to freedom. Burning the map isn't about making a spectacle; it's about rejecting slow death by a thousand small compromises. It's about recognizing that persisting on a false path is far more perilous than wandering without a clear route. Sometimes, you have to release the plan to discover the true purpose. And when you do, the landscape unfolds in ways your old map could never have predicted.

You start finding paths by feel. Not intuition in the airy, ungrounded sense, but in the deep, bodily way. You notice who energizes you. What work brings you alive? Which questions can you not stop asking? You make choices based not on how they look in a five-year projection, but on whether they ring proper right now.

You stop asking, "What's the right move?" and start asking, "What's the real move?"

And you stop needing your choices to make sense to everyone else.

That's another cost of burning the map, social dissonance. People won't understand. They'll question. Some will distance themselves. Others will advise caution, not out of malice, but out of their mapping. They haven't seen what you've seen. They haven't felt the fracture. They'll offer you old compasses, outdated coordinates. You can thank them and keep walking.

This isn't about being anti-structure. Maps have their place. I still use them when I'm entering entirely new domains, technical landscapes, collaborative projects, and logistical challenges. But I hold them lightly. I ask: Is this a tool or a trap? Is this map helping me move, or is it helping me avoid something I need to face?

The answers aren't always clean. But they're honest.

That's what this chapter is really about: honesty. The willingness to admit when the thing that used to serve you no longer does. When the plan has expired. When the narrative you've been living is too small for who you've become.

It takes courage to name that. More to act on it.

But if you do, if you trust yourself enough to discard the map, you might discover something you never planned for: a deeper version of your agency. One that doesn't rely on pre-approved steps. One who knows how to stand at a crossroads with no signs and still move forward, not because the path is clear, but because *you* are.

I think we're all carrying old maps. Some we inherited. Some we built out of survival. Some we etched in panic, hoping they'd keep us from ever feeling lost again. But lost isn't the enemy. Lost is the start of real discovery.

So if you're holding a map right now that feels tight, outdated, or misaligned, hold it up to the light. Ask if it still reflects who you are. And if it doesn't, you know what to do.

There's clarity in the fire.

Let it burn.

# Chapter 20: The Logic of Leap

There's a particular flavor of anxiety that lives just before a leap. Not the slow-simmer kind that hums beneath everyday uncertainty, but the sharp, high-voltage kind that appears when you're standing on the edge of something irreversible. Your body knows it before your brain does—your heart rate spikes. Time dilates. The options narrow to one, and yet you hesitate, not because it's wrong, but because you're crossing into territory that won't allow you to return untouched.

I've come to recognize that hesitation not as weakness, but as reverence. There's something sacred about the space between intention and action, especially when the stakes are real. We don't leap because we're sure; we leap because staying still has become untenable. It's not logic in the spreadsheet sense. It's logic in the existential sense. The kind that says: *something more profound in me needs to move, even if I don't know where I'll land.*

For years, I avoided those moments. I was raised, like most people, to believe in planning, preparation, and the virtue of delay. I was taught to wait until I had more information, more clarity, more consensus. But clarity doesn't arrive the way we hope it will. It rarely shows up with a fanfare and a checklist. It leaks in sideways. A conversation that lingers. A daydream that won't let go. A tension in the chest every time you think about staying the same.

Leaps aren't loud declarations. They're the result of quiet dissonance finally becoming unbearable.

The biggest leaps I've taken never came with certainty. They came with unrest. I left jobs when they looked their best on paper.

I turned down offers I'd once fantasized about. I started over when I didn't yet have a name for what I wanted to build. And each time, people asked the same question: *"But how did you know?"* I didn't. That's the point. You don't know. You feel. You sense. You choose. And then you commit to figuring it out midair.

There is no such thing as a risk-free leap. What there is, if you're lucky, is a moment of alignment strong enough to carry you past your conditioning. A flicker of conviction that overrides your programming. You grab it before it disappears. That's the window. That's when you jump.

The logic of the leap defies conventional calculus. Traditional logic asks: "What is the probability of success?" But leaps ask something different: "What is the cost of not trying?" These are not the same equation. One deals in control. The other deals in freedom.

And freedom is expensive.

Not in the romantic, cinematic way. In the real way. You may lose income. Community. Status. Familiarity. You may gain solitude you didn't expect. You may doubt yourself more in the first few weeks than you ever have before. And if you leap with the expectation that everything will immediately make sense, you will panic because most leaps lead first to liminal space, an in-between that feels like floating, or falling, or both.

I've had to make peace with that in-between. With the not-yet. The ungrounded. The awkward humility of starting over. And the truth is, the longer you delay that discomfort, the heavier the leap becomes. Because the logic doesn't get clearer, it just gets drowned out by more reasons to stay. Comfort calcifies. Rationalization builds. Soon, you're living a life that looks stable but feels suffocating. You're applauded for your consistency while quietly detaching from yourself.

The leap, when it finally comes, isn't heroic. It's corrective.

I'm not saying every risk is worth it. Leaping indiscriminately is just another form of avoidance. The leap has to mean something. It has to speak to a part of you that's been whispering for longer than you've admitted. Sometimes it's a whisper for autonomy. Sometimes for truth. Sometimes for expression. But it's always something primal. Something too vital to ignore indefinitely.

When I reflect on the moments I leapt into new work, new cities, new roles, even new versions of myself, I see one common thread. None of those choices made complete sense from the outside. They didn't match the trajectory people assumed I was on. But they made *internal* sense. They brought me closer to coherence. And coherence, I've learned, is more valuable than clarity.

Coherence occurs when your actions align with your inner state, and you embody it, when you stop needing the leap to look impressive and start needing it to feel real.

That's the logic I trust now. Not the five-year plan. Not the approval. Not the odds. I trust the inner yes that doesn't go away. The ache that sharpens when I delay. The idea I can't unsee. That's the objective metric. If it keeps coming back, it's yours to answer.

Of course, there's always the fear of being wrong and leaping and regretting. But what I've found, again and again, is that even when a leap doesn't "work," it clarifies. It reveals what you needed to learn. It strips away pretense. It wakes up something dormant. You may fall hard, but you don't fall empty. You land with something you didn't have before: evidence of your agency.

And that's worth something.

We live in a world that fetishizes certainty, yet rewards audacity. We are told to optimize, plan, minimize risk, and then we're sold stories of those who defied it all. We praise the leap after it succeeds, but question it in progress. That contradiction can drive you mad unless you remember this: leaps are never validated in advance. They're justified retroactively, if at all.

So don't leap for applause. Don't leap for validation. Leap because staying would be a lie. Because your future self is quietly watching, waiting to see if you'll keep playing safe, or finally bet on something true.

The logic of the leap is not binary. It doesn't promise success. It promises *movement*. And sometimes that's enough. Sometimes that's everything. Because life isn't a problem to be solved, it's a direction to be chosen. And there are places you can only reach by leaving the ground.

Jump.

# Chapter 21: How to Make an Irreversible Decision

There are two kinds of decisions in life: the kind you can walk back and the kind you can't. We pretend most decisions are reversible because that makes them easier to stomach, but the truth is, the ones that shape us, the ones that define what kind of life we get to live, are the ones we can't undo. And that's where things get complicated. Because once you know the decision is irreversible, it's no longer just about logic. It becomes existential.

I used to think irreversibility was a bad thing. That meant committing to something unquestioningly, or burning a bridge you might someday need. But I've since learned it's the only way to move into the next version of yourself. Reversible decisions keep you in loops. They offer the comfort of the exit hatch, but they also dilute your conviction. Irreversible decisions are the ones that force you to grow into who you said you were becoming.

But how do you make them? How do you trust yourself enough to step into a future you can't retreat from?

The first lie we're told is that irreversible decisions require certainty. They don't. They need clarity, but that's a very different thing. Certainty says, "This will work." Clarity says, "This is mine to do, even if it doesn't." That distinction is everything. Certainty is a gamble on the outcome. Clarity is a commitment to the action, regardless of what comes next.

Clarity is quieter. It rarely arrives in the form of a thunderbolt. More often, it trickles in through dissonance, the subtle friction of living out of alignment. You notice the job that feels emptier than it used to. The relationship you're still in is because it's familiar. The version of yourself you've been performing because it's easier than becoming. Clarity starts there, not in a moment of triumph, but in a moment of honesty.

The problem is, our lives are optimized to drown out that kind of honesty. We chase distractions. We crowd our calendars. We turn up the volume on everything but ourselves. Because deep down, we know that absolute clarity usually demands fundamental change. And irreversible change terrifies us, not just because of what we'll lose, but because of who we'll stop being.

There's grief in that, even when the change is good.

No one talks enough about the mourning that accompanies irreversible choices. When you leap, you don't just leave a situation, you leave a self. And if you don't honor that loss, it will haunt you. I've seen people sabotage their progress because they never made peace with the version of themselves they had to let go of. They didn't give themselves time to say goodbye.

So part of making an irreversible decision is grieving in advance. It's acknowledging that the leap comes at a cost, and that the price includes your own identity, not as a punishment, but as a passage.

Once you've done that, once you've felt the weight of what the decision means, you can start asking the right questions. Not "Will this work?" but "Is this true?" Not "What will they think?" but "Can I live with myself if I don't do this?" These questions don't make the decision easier. They make it *real*.

The best irreversible decisions I've made were preceded by internal battles that lasted months, sometimes years. On the outside, the change looked sudden. On the inside, it was the final chapter of a quiet war. I've left cities, ended partnerships, and said no to opportunities that would've changed my financial trajectory. And every time, I did so with a sick feeling in my gut, not because I doubted the move, but because I understood what it meant.

Irreversible means there's no rewind. But it doesn't mean there's no recovery.

We forget that. We think irreversibility equals catastrophe if we're wrong. But there's a subtle difference between irreversible and irredeemable. You may not be able to undo the decision, but you can still grow through it. You can still repair. Rebuild. Realign. The move might be final, but the story isn't.

That's the second thing I've learned: **irreversible doesn't mean you have to get it right**. It just means you have to own it.

Owning it is the real work. There's a kind of power that only comes from cutting off the escape route. The moment you step into something without a Plan B, your posture changes. Your attention sharpens. Your excuses die. You become someone who has no choice but to engage fully, and that's where most transformation happens, not in the moment of the decision, but in the months that follow, when you're forced to live with it.

People avoid irreversible decisions because they think they're too fragile. That if the thing goes sideways, they'll break. But I've found the opposite to be true. We're more resilient than we think. What we lack is practice. Practice living in consequences. Practice navigating regret. Practice finding our footing in terrain we can't reverse out of.

Most of us are overtrained in analysis and undertrained in aftermath.

We're great at forecasting and terrible at integration. We want guarantees instead of capacity. But irreversible decisions don't ask you to know the future; they ask you to *build yourself into someone who can meet it.*

That's the third truth. It's not about the decision. It's about the decider.

You don't make an irreversible choice because you're ready. You make it because the person you need to become won't emerge until after you do. You won't find that version of yourself while hedging. You won't meet them while rehearsing. You'll only meet them in motion, on the other side of no return.

I don't want to romanticize this. Irreversible decisions can wreck things. You can hurt people. You can lose what you didn't intend to. That's why the clarity has to be real. That's why the grief has to be felt. Because if you skip those steps, the leap becomes reckless. But if you honor them, the jump becomes sacred.

It becomes a line you draw not just in your life, but in your identity. A statement: I am willing to bear the consequences of acting on what I know to be true. Even if it costs me. Even if I'm afraid. Even if it means walking a path no one else can walk with me.

This isn't impulsiveness; it's integrity. In a world obsessed with reversibility, where every decision is hedged, every plan overanalyzed, and every commitment postponed, integrity becomes a radical act. So, how do you make an irreversible decision? You begin by stopping the habit of outsourcing the answer. You acknowledge the dissonance within yourself. You allow yourself to grieve what you must leave behind. You confront the questions that demand attention. You listen deeply until clarity, not certainty, emerges. Then you leap, not because you feel sure, but because you can no longer bear to betray yourself. That is how you make a move that can't be undone. You become the version of yourself that no longer needs to look back.

## Chapter 22: The Cost of Momentum

Momentum is a seductive force. Once it starts to build, everything becomes easier to justify, including the workflows. The feedback loops accelerate. You're seen, acknowledged, maybe even celebrated. It feels like confirmation that you're on the right path, and so you keep going and going and going. Until one day, you realize you haven't asked yourself a single honest question in a very long time.

We tend to treat momentum like proof. If things are moving, then they must be moving in the right direction. If others are following, buying, and responding, then we must be doing something worthwhile. But the problem with momentum is that it doesn't ask for consent. It doesn't care whether the direction still feels aligned. It rewards movement for its own sake.

And eventually, it demands obedience.

I've seen it happen in every field. A writer who finally gains traction and keeps producing work that no longer excites them, because the algorithm likes it. A founder who scales faster than they're ready for, and then becomes a hostage of the machine they built. A public thinker whose early insights turn into a performance they can no longer escape. In each case, the common thread is this: momentum became the master.

The most dangerous thing about momentum is that it impersonates clarity. It creates a kind of external gravity, one that feels like purpose but is inertia. You don't want to disrupt it, as doing so might break something fragile. But fragility can hide inside even the most impressive velocity. And when you don't question the momentum, you become the passenger in a vehicle you're no longer steering.

I've had to learn this lesson the hard way.

There was a point when everything I touched seemed to generate traction. The projects were landing. The connections were flowing. The systems were working. But underneath the surface, I was hollowing out. The pace I had established for myself, because it worked, became the very thing that eroded my internal compass. It was only when I stepped back and allowed the momentum to die that I realized how far I had drifted.

Letting it die was brutal.

We don't talk enough about how much courage it takes to interrupt something that's working. To voluntarily slow down, or stop altogether, when the world is telling you to keep going. There's a kind of social gravity in momentum, too, the expectation that once you start, you must never stop. But every system that cannot be paused is already broken.

You don't need to crash to justify a pivot. You don't need to fail to permit yourself to rest. But if you wait until collapse, the decision will be made for you.

Sometimes the cost of momentum is subtle: a quiet disconnection from the work that once mattered. Sometimes it's dramatic: a public burnout, a lost sense of self, a painful severing from something once beloved. And sometimes, it's existential: waking up successful in a life that no longer feels like yours.

Momentum will carry you past the point of meaning if you let it.

So how do you tell when it's time to stop? How do you know if you're riding momentum or being ridden by it?

One sign is when speed replaces reflection. You make decisions faster because you "don't have time" to slow down. You rationalize away discomfort because the stakes feel too high to pause. You prioritize continuity over clarity. You stop listening to the quiet signals that once guided you. In the name of growth, you amputate your awareness.

Another sign is when questions feel threatening. When the idea of asking "Why am I doing this?" or "Do I still believe in this?" feels too destabilizing to consider. That's not clarity. That's fear disguised as progress. And fear makes for a terrible compass.

The paradox of momentum is that it's easiest to question when you don't have it, and hardest to confront when you do. When things are slow, you're forced to introspect. When things are fast, you're incentivized to keep sprinting. But if you don't learn how to pause *while moving*, you'll eventually learn how to break, because you didn't.

The healthiest people I know aren't the ones with the most momentum. They're the ones who can walk away from it.

Not out of laziness. Not because they don't care. But because they understand the difference between performance and truth. They know that *moving toward* something is not the same as *driving through* something. And they have the discipline to choose the more challenging path, the one that may slow them down, but keeps them aligned.

Momentum is a tool. A lever. A signal. But it is not a moral good. It doesn't mean you're doing the right thing. It doesn't mean you're okay. It just means you're moving. And if you're not clear on why, or toward what, then speed is irrelevant.

Extraordinary lives aren't built by rushing forward; they're built by moving with authenticity. Sometimes that means pausing even when you're winning. Sometimes it means dismantling systems you've outgrown. Sometimes it means risking being overlooked to preserve your coherence and integrity. Because the worst kind of momentum is the kind that carries you somewhere you never intended to go. True clarity often reveals itself only in the stillness that follows stopping. Integrity endures when you dare to acknowledge that certain burdens no longer belong to you, no matter how far carrying them has brought you. And peace becomes attainable when you embrace slowing down not as failure, but as an act of authorship. You are not here to obey momentum; you are here to decide where the story goes next.

# Chapter 23: Conviction Without Certainty

I used to think conviction came from proof. Before you could stand firm in your belief, you had to gather overwhelming evidence, gain consensus, and eliminate doubt. But over time, I've learned that the most meaningful conviction doesn't emerge from certainty; it grows despite its absence.

Conviction, as I've come to understand it, is not the same as confidence. It's not bravado, or volume, or dominance in a room. It's quieter than that. It's the calm, stubborn presence that allows you to move forward even when nothing outside of you affirms your decision. It's what you hold onto when the evidence is thin, the path is unclear, and the risk is real, but you move anyway, because not moving would betray something essential in you.

The world doesn't reward this kind of conviction immediately. It often punishes it. People like certainty. They crave predictability. They trust plans with bullet points and timelines. So when you show up with a direction but not a guarantee, a sense of purpose but not a proof, you will be questioned. Sometimes aggressively. Sometimes politely. Sometimes silently, with distance and withdrawal. But make no mistake, when you lead with conviction and not consensus, you threaten the architecture of comfort.

You also threaten your ego. Because conviction without certainty is deeply vulnerable, it means you might be wrong. You might fail. You might embarrass yourself. And the mind is trained to avoid these outcomes. It wants insurance. It wants applause. It seeks the security of being backed by something larger than intuition.

But intuition is no less than data. It's just harder to defend in a spreadsheet. It doesn't speak in charts or metrics. It says in tension and clarity, in quiet unease when you consider compromising, in the inner friction that builds when you deny what you know. That's where conviction starts, not with external validation, but with internal unrest.

There's a moment in every meaningful decision when you stop asking if others see what you see, when you stop needing them to. When the stakes of waiting become heavier than the fear of being alone, that's when conviction crystallizes, not as a certainty that you'll succeed, but as a refusal to betray the truth you carry.

I've made decisions that baffled people—walked away from things that looked ideal on paper—said yes to paths with no defined endpoint. I've been called impulsive, delusional, and even self-sabotaging. And sometimes I've wondered if they were right. But the longer I've followed that inner line, the more I've come to see that conviction isn't about avoiding doubt. It's about *acting anyway*.

In a world obsessed with optimization, conviction looks inefficient. It doesn't follow the flowchart. It doesn't respond to market research. It doesn't always make sense. But sense is not the only compass. Sometimes the thing you're building doesn't exist yet. Sometimes the path only becomes visible because you walked it first. And if you wait for others to believe before you begin, you'll be trapped in an endless loop of hesitation.

Conviction is a precondition for emergence. It creates space where something new can come into being. And it's rarely dramatic. Often it's just the decision to keep showing up. To keep doing the work when no one's watching. To keep returning to the task, the idea, the belief that won't let go of you, even when it's inconvenient. Especially when it's problematic.

There's a difference between being stubborn and being rooted. Stubbornness resists feedback. Rootedness listens but doesn't sway easily. Conviction without certainty requires the latter. It asks you to stay open to new information, to adapt, to evolve, but not to abandon what brought you here in the first place.

This balance is fragile. Tip too far toward doubt, and you collapse under the weight of uncertainty. Tip too far toward arrogance, and you lose the ability to learn. Conviction lives in that middle tension, the willingness to proceed without complete understanding, but not without reflection.

I think of all the people who've made things that matter—the ones we now see as visionaries. Most of them were misunderstood at first. They weren't applauded for their clarity; they were doubted for their deviation. But they had conviction, not because they were sure of the outcome, but because they couldn't do otherwise. They weren't gambling. They were answering.

We often mistake that for ego. But absolute conviction doesn't inflate the self, it empties it. It puts you in the service of something larger than comfort. Larger than reputation. It demands humility, not certainty. Because you're not clinging to being right. You're committing to what feels *right enough to try*.

That distinction liberates you. Once you let go of the need for certainty, you stop waiting and cease putting your life on hold for perfect information. You come to understand that it is movement, not mastery, that hones your grasp of truth. Learning happens through action, clarity emerges through doing, and refinement is born from experience. Conviction is not an innate trait but something nurtured each time you choose to follow your compass in the absence of a clear map. The world doesn't need more people frozen in hesitation; it needs more people willing to act from alignment, even amidst uncertainty and messiness. It needs those who can say, "I don't know exactly where this leads, but I know it begins here." It requires individuals who are prepared to lead themselves. Conviction, at its core, is self-leadership under pressure, not about dominance or bravado, but the quiet, persistent discipline of living honestly when surrendering would be easier. You don't need absolute certainty to move forward; you only need the courage to walk alone if you must, to listen intently, act with clarity, and adapt with bravery, treading the delicate line between courage and humility, time and again.

# Chapter 24: The Weight of Watching Eyes

There's a shift that happens when people start paying attention. You can feel it in your posture, in the hesitation before you speak, in the invisible calculation that starts to filter what you say and do. It begins subtly. A raised eyebrow from someone you respect. A few more followers on your social accounts. A project is gaining traction. And then, before you know it, your decisions stop being yours alone.

This is the weight of watching eyes.

It's the gravitational pull of perception. The awareness that you're being seen, evaluated, judged, sometimes praised, sometimes scrutinized, but always *observed*. And unless you're careful, that awareness starts to shape your choices. You don't just do the work anymore. You perform the role. You narrate your process. You frame your experience for consumption, validation, or defense. You stop creating from curiosity and start producing for applause.

I don't say this as a critique. I say it as someone who's fallen into it more than once. The first time I shared something that resonated, I felt a jolt of affirmation. That electric sense of being understood, of connecting. It was addictive. And then came the pressure to maintain it. To say more of what worked, and less of what didn't. To be consistent. Predictable. Branded.

This is how identity calcifies, not through failure, but through success. You do something that hits, and people respond. Then you start doing it because of the response, not because it's still true. That's when it starts to hollow. That's when you begin living a version of yourself shaped by how others see you, rather than how you feel in your skin.

And it's subtle, this shift. It's not a switch you flip. It's a thousand tiny recalibrations. You soften a statement here. You hold back a change in direction there. You hesitate to admit uncertainty because your audience has come to expect clarity. Before long, you're no longer leading your life; you're curating it. And that curation becomes a cage.

The watching eyes are not always malicious. Often, they're admiring. Well-meaning. They love what you've done. They want more of it. But that love can become a leash. The moment your identity becomes tied to their expectations, you lose the freedom to evolve.

This is where many people freeze.

They stop experimenting. They stop changing their minds. They stop being wrong in public. And when you stop doing those things, you stop growing. Because growth is messy. Evolution is inconsistent. And becoming who you are requires disappointing people who loved who you were.

The hardest thing about visibility is that it tempts you to prioritize continuity over authenticity.

When I've been at my worst, it was usually because I was trying to preserve an image. I wasn't lying, but I wasn't telling the whole truth either. I was editing my experience to match a narrative I thought people needed from me. That kind of editing is soul-numbing. It turns your life into a performance. And the more you perform, the less you remember who you were before the stage lights turned on.

To reclaim yourself, you have to be willing to disappoint.

Not out of spite. Not recklessly. But deliberately. You have to accept that some people will misunderstand your pivots. Some will see your silence as inconsistency. Some will interpret your evolution as betrayal. And still, you have to move.

Because the alternative is stagnation, the alternative is betraying *yourself* to protect a reputation that's already out of your hands. You can't control how people receive you. You can only control whether you're being real.

And here's the paradox: the more real you are, the more magnetic your work becomes. Not in the short-term, algorithmic sense. But in a more profound understanding. The enduring sense. The kind that resonates beyond trend or moment. The type that isn't easily shaken, because it's rooted in something more than performance.

This doesn't mean you owe the world your rawness. You don't have to bleed on cue or disclose every insecurity. Boundaries matter—privacy matters. But there's a difference between protecting your inner life and protecting your public persona. One is healthy. The other is suffocating.

You don't have to be fearless. But you do have to be faithful to your pulse, your process, your unfolding. That's what watching eyes can never fully see. They see the artifacts, not the becoming. They know the result, not the wrestling. That's why you must be your witness first. Because if you're not, the applause will trick you into thinking you've arrived somewhere permanent.

Nothing is permanent. The person you are today won't be the same in five years, or even five months. If you're moving forward honestly, you'll look back at some of your past beliefs with discomfort; that's a sign you're still alive and evolving. It's not the watching eyes that hinder us; the real challenge is when we let them dictate our story. Permit yourself to change openly, to grow in full view, even if it confuses those who thought they understood you. Allow yourself to pivot in the middle of sentences, projects, or life itself. Be seen as a work in progress, not just a finished product. Those who truly matter will stay alongside you; those who don't were never there for you, they were there for the version of you that maintained their comfort. Let go of them. Let go of the performance. And continually return to that inner place that never sought permission to begin. That is where the real work happens. That is where the next chapter starts.

## Chapter 25: The Quiet Exit

Not all endings are dramatic. Some things happen quietly that you don't notice until long after they've passed. A conversation that slowly loses heat. A habit you stop returning to. A place that no longer feels like home. We're conditioned to expect exits to be loud, marked by declarations, conflict, or finality. But the most honest exits I've ever made didn't announce themselves. They whispered.

And often, they whispered for months before I dared to listen.

The quiet exit isn't a failure of boldness. It's a form of integrity. It means you've outgrown something, and instead of burning it down or dragging it out, you walk away. No spectacle. No resentment. No need for vindication. Just a clean, respectful release.

But here's the catch: quiet exits aren't always easy to justify. Because they don't come with clear villains, they rarely offer external validation. You can't always explain them in a sentence. Sometimes all you can say is, *This is no longer for me.* And if you're someone who's used to offering reasons, the absence of a tangible "why" can make you feel dishonest, even when you're being more truthful than ever.

I've exited friendships, businesses, cities, and roles, all without blowouts or fanfare. I left because staying would've meant shrinking. Because the cost of continuation had shifted from effort to erosion. Because I realized that peace isn't always found through fixing, it's seen through leaving.

But society doesn't reward quiet exits. It rewards endurance. It romanticizes the fight. It teaches us to try harder, stay longer, push through. Walking away without a visible wound can be seen as a weakness, especially if things looked fine on the outside. And so, we stay. Not because it's right, but because it's legible. Justifiable. Palatable to others.

This is where people get stuck.

They confuse momentum with meaning. They conflate obligation with purpose. They fear being misunderstood more than they fear being misaligned. And so, they wait, for a dramatic break, for a definitive sign, for permission. But the most critical exits rarely wait for perfect timing. They arrive as a quiet truth. And the longer you ignore that truth, the more it costs you.

There is a moment when silence becomes clarity.

You stop trying to force a feeling. You stop waiting for things to return to how they were. You stop bargaining with your disinterest. And then, in that stillness, something shifts. You realize that leaving doesn't require anger. It doesn't need to be framed as a rebellion. It can be a simple decision to stop pouring energy into something that no longer reflects you.

And that's terrifying.

Because it's hard to leave when nothing is technically wrong, when the job is stable, the relationship is functional, and the project is profitable. But not mistaken is not the same as right. Neutrality is not vitality. And if you settle for the absence of pain, you'll never experience the presence of aliveness.

The quiet exit is a vote for aliveness.

It says, "I don't need this to be broken to choose something better." It trusts the signal without demanding proof. It lets go with grace, not out of indifference but out of respect, for the path, for the self, for the evolution unfolding.

There is a profound dignity in choosing stillness rather than stagnation. Yet, it is essential not to confuse the quiet exit with emotional detachment. Leaving, especially when it is the right choice, is accompanied by grief. This grief stems not only from departing a situation but from letting go of a part of yourself: a familiar rhythm, a long-held story. Releasing that narrative without assigning blame or seeking a villain represents one of the most mature acts a person can undertake. Despite this, others will inevitably ask questions: Why did you stop? Why now? What happened?

And often, your answer will be soft. Incomplete. It won't satisfy their curiosity. And that's okay. You're not obligated to offer a post-mortem on your own. Not every exit requires an essay. Sometimes the most valid reason is: *I'm choosing myself.* And sometimes even that doesn't need to be said out loud.

I think we underestimate how many quiet exits we've already made.

The ones from identities we no longer try to prove. From opinions we no longer defend. From roles we no longer feel the need to perform. We don't call those exits, but they are. They're the slow, invisible ways we reclaim our energy. They matter just as much as the big breaks.

There is another crucial aspect to consider. Quiet exits aren't always about external circumstances; often, they occur internally, when you stop resisting reality, release the need to control how others perceive you, or let go of beliefs that once limited your growth. These internal departures are invisible to others, yet they transform everything. They create space, relax the body, clear the mind, and open the way for new movement. The quiet exit is far from passive or a form of surrender. It is a deliberate choice to align yourself without demand, drama, or delay. It is an act of sovereignty, a subtle and steady reclaiming of your agency. If you find yourself at the edge of something that no longer fits, hearing only a whisper where you expected a roar, take this as your permission to listen. You don't need applause, a breakdown, or a justification that satisfies everyone else. What you need to recognize is that your presence is a powerful resource, and you alone decide where it will be directed.

# Chapter 26: The Edge of Enough

There's a strange silence that comes after you get what you thought you wanted. You push, you strive, you chase the thing, the position, the income, the influence, the security, and then one day, it arrives. You hit the milestone. You reach the goal. And instead of elation, you feel… something else. Not emptiness exactly, but a disorienting calm. A question that hangs in the air: *now what?*

This is the edge of enough.

It's a place most people never expect to reach, let alone learn how to inhabit, because we're taught to crave growth. Not just growth, but expansion, more audience, more income, more opportunity, more relevance. Enough isn't celebrated. It's assumed to be a pit stop, a fleeting moment before you set your sights higher. We don't rest enough. We leverage it.

And yet, there's something profound about arriving at that quiet line, the recognition that more might not add meaning, that enough might not be a plateau, but a horizon. That's when the real questions begin, not about acquisition, but about authorship.

Because if you're no longer chasing survival or validation or arrival, then what are you here to do?

That question unnerves people, especially the high achievers, the ones who've always measured progress in motion. When you've spent your life reaching, pausing can feel like failure. And in a culture built on ambition, maintaining a certain level of success can feel like mediocrity. But that's a distortion. Enough does not mean stagnation; rather, it represents a threshold, an entry point where genuine intentionality can begin. There is a subtle but vital skill in learning when to stop expanding, in protecting the capacity you have carefully earned, and in guarding the space that your success has made possible. Once you have built a life that genuinely meets your needs, the nature of your work changes. It is no longer about relentless scaling or accumulation but about stewardship, maintaining and defending the integrity of what you have created. It becomes about saying no, not from a place of fear or limitation, but from a place of fidelity: fidelity to the life you designed, to the rhythms that sustain you, and to the priorities that your success was meant to serve.

Most people blow past that line.

They don't know how to recognize it when they feel it. Or they don't trust it. Or they're terrified that if they stop reaching, they'll lose their edge. So, they keep going. Not because they need more, but because they're afraid of what stillness might reveal.

That's when enough becomes invisible. When it gets buried beneath the next offer, the following metric is the next urgent opportunity. And before long, you've sacrificed the peace you built in service of a version of yourself you no longer are.

I've done it.

I've watched my sense of enough slip away without realizing how to honor it. I kept growing, pushing, and saying yes simply because I could, because opportunities kept arriving and the momentum never slowed. Eventually, I looked up and saw that I had accumulated more than I needed, yet had less of what I initially sought. This is the paradox: more opportunity, but less time; more recognition, but less privacy; more leverage, but less stillness. I came to understand that if you don't define your boundary enough, someone else will, usually in the form of external pressures like expectations, algorithms, markets, or audiences. These forces don't care about your peace; they care only about your output, your relevance, and your ability to produce. You must draw your line and then defend it every day. You have to practice saying, "I could do more, but I won't." You must become comfortable with being misunderstood, with walking away from opportunities that exceed your needs but threaten your design, and with appearing smaller than you are to maintain your sanity. There is real courage in that.

Because everything around you will tell you to keep climbing, that enough is a myth. That if you don't expand, you'll disappear. But that's fear talking—scarcity disguised as strategy. The truth is, enough isn't static; it evolves. It's not a number or a finish line. It's a felt sense. A deep knowing that your life, as it is, can hold you.

Living at the edge of enough demands a kind of discipline that reshapes how we measure success. It means moving away from the relentless chase for constant relevance and instead embracing sustained resonance, prioritizing coherence over fleeting attention. This shift asks us to optimize not for growth alone, but for grace in how we live and lead. Most importantly, it requires trusting that stepping back is not falling behind; instead, it is falling into a natural rhythm that honors our limits and values. The edge of enough does not mark the end of ambition. Still, it signals its transformation, a reorientation from proving ourselves to preserving what truly matters, from accumulating more to authoring our lives with intentionality, and from speed to depth.

At this point, dreaming doesn't cease; it simply evolves. Dreams become more localized, more intimate, and more honest. They no longer seek applause but instead nurture a sense of aliveness that sustains us. If you feel the subtle pull suggesting that what you have is sufficient, that the next step forward might not be upward but inward and deeper, pay attention. Resist the noise that equates to failure or stagnation. Enough is a conscious choice, a refusal to let life be endlessly scaled or measured by external metrics. It is a reclaiming of the very purpose behind the climb, a place where performance gives way to presence, and where authentic living begins.

## Chapter 27: The Season of Stillness

There comes a point when the path forward stops being about what you build, chase, or fix, and starts being about what you *can finally allow to rest*. The impulse to act has its place. Motion carries us through uncertainty. Action becomes the antidote to fear. But there is a danger in staying there too long. When momentum becomes habit, and movement becomes the only acceptable state, you lose the capacity to hear what silence has been trying to tell you.

Stillness is not the absence of progress. It's the recalibration of it. We are wired to associate stillness with stagnation, and we forget it's where the most meaningful recalculations happen. But stillness is not neutral. It has a posture, a structure, and a weight. It doesn't come naturally to those of us who have survived by staying busy. It feels unfamiliar, like a tool we were never properly trained to wield.

I used to believe that rest was what you earned *after* the real work was done. That quiet was a luxury afforded to those who had solved their chaos. I waited for my life to settle enough to invite stillness in. But I was wrong. Stillness isn't what happens after the work; it *is* the work. It's not passive. It demands intention. It reveals what activity can obscure.

What I didn't realize at first is that stillness doesn't just settle the nervous system; it exposes what's unresolved. When the noise drops out and the external demands fade, what's left is a raw confrontation with yourself. That's why so many people avoid it. The surface calm is easy to romanticize, but beneath it, stillness strips away the scaffolding. If you've been performing, you'll feel the hollowness. If you've been avoiding the grief, it will surface. If you've been compensating, the fatigue will catch up.

But that's the point.

Stillness is diagnostic. It tells the truth without shouting. You begin to notice which thoughts won't quiet themselves. You start to feel where your body holds tension you never permitted it to release. You remember dreams you buried under practicality. And slowly, you begin to understand the shape of your own life again, not as a project to manage, but as a terrain to tend.

There is a season for that. And when it comes, you will have to decide whether you will honor it.

You may feel it as exhaustion that no sleep can fix. A subtle resistance to activities you used to enjoy. A growing sense that your output no longer matches your inner state. These aren't signs of failure. They're signals. And they often mean one thing: it's time to stop *for a while*.

This is where the tension shows up. In a culture obsessed with optimization, a deliberate slowing feels radical. You'll wonder if you're being lazy. You'll worry that you're losing ground. The world will keep moving, and part of you will ache to rejoin the race. But that's precisely why this season matters. Because stillness isn't a withdrawal from life, it's a deepening into it.

Not everything improves through acceleration. Not every breakthrough comes from grinding. Some truths only arrive when you stop pushing, when you clear the noise. When you permit yourself to sit with what is, not what should be, or what could be, but what *is*. And in that space, something subtle begins to grow. A steadiness. A clarity. A sense of internal weight that doesn't require explanation or defense.

The world won't validate your stillness. It rewards hustle. It amplifies visibility. It commodifies momentum. But those who learn to inhabit the quiet, who treat stillness not as an escape but as a responsibility, begin to carry a different kind of power. Not louder, but deeper. Not faster, but truer.

In my own life, I've come to understand stillness not as a weakness or a pause in progress, but as a kind of seasonal intelligence, an essential rhythm of preparation rather than failure. Just as nature enters its quiet seasons without apology, so too must we accept our own need for rest without judgment. Trees shed their leaves in autumn without hesitation, soil lies dormant beneath the surface, and the sky holds still on calm days; none of these natural cycles require explanation or justification. Yet, unlike the world around us, we often pathologize stillness, fearing it as a sign of defeat or inertia. But what if we approached it differently? What if, rather than waiting until we are completely drained, we learned to recognize stillness as a necessary phase and built rituals to honor it? What if stillness, like any other season, had its form of productivity, not measured in visible output but in the deep work of integration? Integration is the process of weaving together the lessons we have hurried past, distilling chaos into clarity, and reconnecting with parts of ourselves that relentless achievement has long silenced. Without this integration, even the most carefully made decisions remain fragile, carried out by fragmented minds and exhausted bodies. Stillness has the power to bring those fragments home. It is the space where wisdom finally catches up, where the relentless chase for worthiness subsides because you have made room to remember it. It is the moment when you stop striving to earn clarity and instead open yourself to receive it.

And yes, it is uncomfortable at first. Especially if you've built your identity on usefulness, but once you stop equating stillness with irrelevance, you realize it's the only place from which actual authorship can emerge. You can't write a new chapter if you never pause to turn the page.

If you're feeling the pull toward quiet, still mornings, closed calendars, and deeper breaths, don't wait for the world to permit you. Take it and take it seriously. Stillness isn't a retreat; it's a rehearsal for re-entry. When the season ends, and it will, you'll emerge not just rested but rewired, not slower, just more precise, and that clarity will change everything you touch next.

# Chapter 28: When the Future Stops Asking for You

There's a peculiar kind of silence that arrives when the future stops making demands. For most of our lives, the future is noisy. It prods, it pressures, it whispers its expectations in our ears, become this, do that, prepare for this. It tugs at our decisions, shapes our routines, and gives our anxiety a place to live. We spend years running toward it, designing ourselves to be legible to it, grooming our lives to make sense in some imagined tomorrow. But eventually, if we're paying attention, we reach a point where the future doesn't call the shots anymore.

This is not a defeat. It's a liberation. But it doesn't feel like that at first.

It begins with disorientation. The goals that once gave shape to your days start to lose their urgency. The roles you performed well begin to feel like costumes you forgot to take off. The calendar thins, and not just because of a scheduling app. It thins because you stop building a life around the assumption that more is coming, more status, more relevance, more time, more proof that you mattered.

For years, the future was architecture. You measured decisions by how they paid off down the road. You delayed gratification. You made bets. You chased long arcs. You traded now for later. And then one day, it stops being the goal. Not because life ends, but because your orientation shifts. You're no longer trying to impress the future. You're trying to be honest with the present.

That moment is unsettling. Because much of our identity is woven into who we might become. When that scaffolding drops away, what's left is something simpler, and therefore scarier: who we are, right now, without projection.

What happens when you no longer aspire to become?

What happens when the ladder disappears and the path becomes a field?

When the only one asking you to prove anything is the voice you thought you'd outgrown?

There's grief in this. The grief of putting down tools you've carried since youth. The grief of realizing some dreams were scaffolds, not destinations. The grief of being honest about how much you sacrificed to appease a future that, in hindsight, was never going to applaud you.

And still, this isn't an ending. It's the emergence of another kind of authorship.

When the future stops asking for you, something extraordinary becomes possible. You stop deferring your life to some hypothetical arrival. You begin to inhabit your hours differently. Food tastes more vivid. Conversations become more textured. The body becomes less of a machine and more of a home.

But you also lose excuses. You can no longer say, "One day." That phrase doesn't belong here anymore. What's left is the question: "If not now, then why not?" And there's no abstraction to hide behind. There's only the moment, and your relationship to it. That's where meaning starts to become something you make, not something you chase.

I've seen people unravel at this threshold. Not because they've failed, but because they didn't know how to live without the future performing for them. They needed an audience. They required the arc. They needed the promise that their sacrifice would be noticed. When that promise goes quiet, so do they.

But others, those who've done the deeper work of severing identity from ambition, step into something more potent. They stop trying to shape time and instead let it shape them. They slow down. They listen more. They stop managing their lives like portfolios. They live in questions without needing answers.

And oddly, this is where their work becomes most honest.

Because there's nothing to sell anymore. No image to curate. No brand to defend. Just attention. Just intention. Just presence.

You might assume that this place, the one where the future stops asking for you, is where you fade. But the opposite often happens. You become luminous in a different way. You start saying things no one else can tell, because you're no longer trying to compete. You take risks that once felt unimaginable, because you're no longer mortgaging your spirit for security. You become more dangerous, in the best sense, because you're finally free.

There's no instruction manual for this transition. It's not a life stage so much as a shift in gravity. It can happen at thirty, or sixty, or not at all. Some people never stop being useful to the future, and they confuse that utility for meaning. But others choose to let that economy collapse. They stop contorting themselves to fit narratives of progress and begin crafting narratives of coherence.

There's a sacredness to that decision.

Because it doesn't reject ambition, it refines it. It asks, "What do I still want, not because it completes me, but because it aligns with me?" It doesn't mean you stop building. It means you stop building for projection and start building for presence.

This is what I wish more people understood about uncertainty.

It's not always about risk mitigation or hedging. Sometimes uncertainty arrives as stillness. As a release. As a door quietly closed on the part of you that needed to be seen to believe you were real. And when that door closes, another opens. One that leads inward, toward a life that no longer needs to be validated to feel vital.

If you find yourself in that place, if the future isn't asking anymore, if the calls have quieted, if the dream feels less urgent, that doesn't mean you're lost. It means you're being invited to stop outsourcing your imagination. To stop leasing your soul to the next five-year plan. To ask yourself what would be worth doing if no one ever saw it but you.

Because that's where absolute freedom lives, not in being seen, but in being whole.

# Chapter 29: Nonlinear Belonging

Belonging, as it's usually described, has always felt like a place you arrive at after meeting certain conditions. Speak the language. Follow the rules. Share the customs. Agree with the group. Once you've adjusted enough and polished the parts of yourself that don't quite fit, you're permitted in. And once you're in, the bargain is simple: stay consistent. Stay knowable. Stay loyal. That's the price of inclusion.

But real belonging, the kind that nourishes you rather than flattens you, doesn't follow that script. It doesn't move in straight lines. It isn't built on conformity or comfort. It is nonlinear. It is unpredictable. It sometimes arrives through contradiction, not cohesion. And when you start to live from a place of deeper integrity, when you begin choosing alignment over approval, you realize that the belonging you've been chasing isn't always the belonging you need.

There's a loneliness that comes with that realization. Not the loneliness of isolation, but the loneliness of recognition: that some of the spaces you've fought to stay in were never built to hold the version of you you're becoming. The friends who knew your ambition may not know your rest. The people who admired your certainty may not recognize your questions. The community that cheered for your growth might not know what to do with your stillness.

You learn this the hard way. Through mismatches. Through misinterpretation. Through invitations that stop arriving. You know it in the silence that follows a new truth you speak aloud, and the silence that follows when no one echoes it back. And it can feel like betrayal. But often, it's just dissonance. The natural drift that occurs when your inner world begins to outpace the outer contexts you've inhabited.

That's where nonlinear belonging begins, not as a replacement for community, but as a deeper relationship to self. A way of anchoring that doesn't require mirroring. A form of orientation that doesn't rely on sameness. It's not about finding your people. It's about becoming the kind of person who no longer has to disappear to stay connected.

That shift doesn't happen all at once. At first, you keep trying to explain yourself. To justify your changes. To soften your honesty so it won't cause friction. But over time, you learn the difference between being misunderstood and being erased. One is tolerable. The other is intolerable. And you start to choose silence over distortion, not out of retreat, but out of sovereignty.

This is where a strange kind of freedom takes root. Because when belonging is no longer contingent on being the version of yourself others expect, you begin to feel a different type of presence. You stop scanning the room for cues. You stop editing your expression. You stop strategizing your identity. You start speaking from the body, not the brand.

That kind of presence is rare. And because it's rare, it often disrupts the systems around it. Your honesty becomes inconvenient. Your ambiguity is threatening. Your refusal to pick a side is seen as betrayal by both. But you begin to understand that true belonging isn't found in agreement. It's found in mutual permission. The ability to be with, without needing to be *of*.

That permission, when mutual, is sacred. It creates spaces where contradiction isn't punished, where questions don't need to be resolved immediately, where growth doesn't threaten the bond. These spaces are rare, but they are real. And you don't find them by fitting in. You find them by showing up whole and letting the people who can hold that version of you reveal themselves.

Until that happens, there will be a liminal space. Seasons where you feel untethered. Times when you belong to no one group, no clear ideology, no fixed identity. It will feel like failure. Like you've lost your place. But that space is not a void. It's a laboratory. It's where the self grows teeth, where you stop outsourcing your sense of reality to consensus, where you learn to trust your pulse more than the crowd's applause.

And then, something subtle begins to occur. You stop chasing certainty. You no longer require resonance in every conversation. You start to hold multiple truths at once. You notice that you can feel lonely *and* liberated. Disoriented *and* at peace. Unrooted *and* whole. That paradox becomes your new ground.

And that's when nonlinear belonging reveals itself, not as a destination, but as a rhythm. You start finding people who've made similar exits. Who've refused similar bargains. They don't need you to shrink. They don't require you to stay static. They don't mistake your evolution for disloyalty. They greet you with curiosity, not confusion. And suddenly, you realize you've entered a new kind of circle—one where coherence matters more than consistency. One where transformation doesn't threaten connection, it deepens it.

But even then, you're not done. Belonging is never final. It ebbs and reforms. It grows and recedes. And the moment you begin to believe it's secure, life will ask you to let go again. Not because you're failing, but because you're still unfolding. And any belonging that can't move with you isn't yours to carry forward.

So you learn to hold it lightly. To cherish connection without clinging. To celebrate resonance without demanding permanence. To let the map redraw itself when your shape changes. And in doing so, you become someone who belongs *first* to yourself.

That's the anchor. That's the quiet strength you carry into every room. The sense that, even if no one nods, you won't disappear. Even if no one affirms, you won't betray. Even if no one stays, you'll still be home.

# Chapter 30: Closing the Loop

Most people don't realize how many open loops they carry. An unfinished conversation. A question that was never answered. A decision that was deferred many times calcified into a kind of ambient guilt. These loops aren't always dramatic. Often, they're quiet, half-thoughts, unresolved tensions, lingering maybes. But they cost energy. They leak clarity. And when too many accumulate, they blur your inner signal. You start living reactively, chasing a resolution that never arrives, weighed down by invisible threads tugging at your attention.

We like to believe we can move on. That time will close the loops for us. That if we ignore what's unresolved long enough, it will decay into irrelevance. But time isn't a cleaner. It's a spotlight. What you don't resolve grows louder, not quieter. It finds its way into your body. Into your tone. Into the subtle ways you hold back or overcompensate. Unclosed loops don't just linger; they replicate. And eventually, they become your baseline.

That's when you forget what clarity feels like. You confuse numbness for calm. You adapt to a kind of chronic unfinishedness. You normalize dissonance. And in doing so, you erode the very thing you need most to navigate uncertainty: an unfragmented self.

Closing the loop isn't about control. It's about coherence. It's not about resolving every conflict or completing every task. It's about reclaiming authorship over your attention. About saying, *this thing is still open, do I want it to be?* Sometimes, closure requires action. A call. A conversation. A decision. Other times, it's internal. A choice to accept that a particular answer may never come, and that peace can exist even without explanation.

One of the most liberating things I ever learned was that I could close a loop without waiting for external permission. I could forgive without reconciliation. I could let go without certainty. I could stop rehearsing a moment I wish had gone differently. I could declare something complete, not because it was tidy, but because I was ready to move beyond it.

That's not denial. That's authorship.

But it takes practice because we're conditioned to leave loops open. To defer. To hold space for possibilities that no longer serve us. We tell ourselves we're being patient when often we're just avoiding discomfort. We keep doors ajar out of obligation. We hold back closure out of fear it will be interpreted as selfishness, or worse, apathy. But the longer we wait, the heavier it all becomes.

There's a myth that open loops make us available. That staying open means staying expansive. But openness without discernment is diffusion. It's how you become porous in ways that exhaust you. Closing the loop doesn't shrink you; it sharpens you. It gives you an edge in time and presence again. You stop scattering. You start choosing.

I've come to think of this process as a kind of energetic bookkeeping. Every unresolved thing is a line item. Every conversation you keep rehearsing, every "maybe later" that keeps slipping, every project you've ghosted but can't quite release, all of it creates cognitive debt. And just like financial debt, it accrues interest. It taxes your capacity to show up where you are now entirely.

The work boils down to taking inventory. Ask what you're still holding onto. Notice the things that revisit you in quiet moments. Notice what you avoid. Then, slowly, deliberately, start closing the loops. Not all at once. But enough that your attention can return to its full strength. Enough that your yes starts to mean something again.

And when you begin this work, something subtle shifts. Your intuition gets louder. Your emotions get clearer. You stop confusing urgency with importance. You start to discern between what's simply old and what's still true. That distinction is what most people never learn to make.

It's possible to close a loop without closure in the traditional sense. You don't need the other person to apologize. You don't need to understand exactly why it ended. You don't need the perfect final moment. You need to decide that you're done giving it rent-free access to your inner space. And when you do, you'll be surprised how quickly the fog begins to lift.

Some loops are rituals that were never meant to last this long. Patterns of over-functioning. Scripts of performance. Identities that once kept you safe now hold you back. These are the hardest to close because they're woven into your self-concept. But even here, closure is possible. You don't destroy these parts. You thank them. You recognize their service. And then you release them, not with aggression, but with gratitude. That's how you exit a version of yourself without violence.

Closing the loop isn't an endpoint; it's a return to presence. In a world obsessed with what's next, it's a deliberate act of discipline to say: before I move forward, I'll finish what I've left undone. This isn't about tidiness; it's about sovereignty, the ability to move without dragging half-finished stories behind you. It's choosing clarity over complexity, not because complexity is wrong, but because clarity allows you to move without contradiction. And in uncertain times, that clarity is everything. The fewer open loops you carry, the more responsive you become. You stop recycling old scripts and start meeting life as it is, unburdened by the past. That's what it means to close the loop: to say, "I've given this enough," to let go of the noise, and to move forward carrying only what's truly yours.

# Chapter 31: The Debrief We Avoid

It's always easier to act than to reflect. Movement protects us from reflection. It gives us something to point to, a rhythm to hide behind. In the aftermath of any decision, especially one made under uncertainty, there's a brief window where clarity is within reach. But instead of sitting in that stillness, most of us pivot immediately to the next move, the next fix, the next effort. We rarely stop to ask, *What just happened?* Not because we don't care, but because the answers might cost us more than we're ready to pay.

We're conditioned to evaluate decisions by outcomes. If it worked, it was good. If it didn't, it wasn't. But that binary logic only works in a world without complexity. In reality, the feedback loop between action and consequence is noisy. You can make the right call and still get burned. You can wing it and still win. And so, the postmortem — the real, uncomfortable, surgical examination of what went down — is both necessary and neglected.

I avoided debriefs for years. I didn't call them that, of course. I didn't revisit things that didn't sit right with me. I'd feel the edge of a mistake, a misjudgment, a failure of nerve, but I'd smother it under activity. I told myself I didn't have time. It was better to keep moving. That reflection was a luxury. But really, I was afraid. Afraid of what I'd find if I paused long enough to see myself.

Because real debriefs don't flatter you. They don't coddle your ego. They hold up a mirror and say: *This part? You missed it. That moment? You avoided the truth. That outcome? It was preventable.* They ask you to feel the weight of your agency, not as punishment, but as authorship. The debrief isn't a courtroom. It's a classroom. But only if you're willing to stay in the seat.

Most of us aren't.

We want closure without confrontation. We want to feel better, not understand better. So, we rush past the reckoning. We minimize, we deflect, we point outward. Or worse, we moralize. We say things like "Everything happens for a reason," not because we believe it, but because it's easier than sitting in the ache of not knowing why something failed.

But the ache is where the gold is.

The point of a debrief isn't to assign blame; it's to extract intelligence. Every uncertain decision leaves residue. Emotional. Strategic. Relational. And if you don't examine it, it hardens into a distortion. You start concluding unresolved pain. You start crafting strategies around old fear. You start seeing patterns where there are none. The next time you're asked to decide under pressure, you're not just reacting to the situation; you're reacting to the ghosts of decisions past.

This is why ritualized reflection matters—it's not indulgent, it's preventative. A structured debrief clears your mental windshield, resets your internal compass, and lets you return to decisions with less drama and more discipline. But to reflect well, you need to build the muscle of honesty and learn to ask sharper questions: What was I trying to protect? Where did I override my instincts? What signal did I miss by rushing? What fear took the wheel—and when? And maybe most importantly: What part of me wasn't ready to know what I now understand? These aren't throwaway prompts. They demand space, and a kind of honesty that doesn't punish but clarifies. Because the goal isn't self-judgment—it's self-clarity. And clarity doesn't come from being perfect; it comes from noticing the pattern. If you never pause to see the pattern, you'll keep calling every mistake a one-off.

That's how you lose agency.

I've worked with leaders who pride themselves on speed, who make brilliant calls under pressure, and yet, they keep bleeding in the same places. Not because they lack insight, but because they've never built a ritual around looking back. They gather their teams for planning, for forecasting, for launching, but never for debriefing. They know how to act. They've forgotten how to metabolize consequence.

But I've also seen the opposite. People who stop, even briefly, after every significant move. Who asks: *What surprised us? What hurt more than we expected? What success didn't feel as good as we thought it would?* These aren't metrics. They're memory work. They build resilience, not just strategy. And over time, they compound into a kind of lived wisdom that no book can teach.

Debriefing amid uncertainty is inherently more challenging because the information available is often unclear and conflicting. It's rare to have a straightforward cause-and-effect to analyze or a definitive answer about what succeeded. Yet, this ambiguity is precisely why reflection matters, not to confirm correctness but to build capacity for better decisions in the future. Sometimes, the loop you need to close isn't about tactics or strategy; it's about emotion. You must examine not only the outcome but also the cost, what the decision took from you in terms of trust, time, confidence, and relationships. Even necessary choices with positive results can leave behind a residue, and if unacknowledged, that burden carries into your subsequent decisions, dulling your courage and belief in yourself. Instead of only asking what happened, ask what the experience did to you. What did it teach you about how you manage uncertainty? Which parts of yourself were present, and which held back? If you find yourself avoiding these questions, pay close attention; resistance often points to the most profound insights. That's where the pain lies, but also where the treasure is hidden. The debrief you most resist is usually the one you need the most, and the longer you postpone it, the more your internal map warps. Close the loop, even if it hurts, and especially if it hurts.

# Chapter 32: Scar Tissue and Signal

There's a kind of memory the body keeps that no calendar can track. It's the memory of rupture, of stress survived, risks taken, decisions made under pressure. You don't always remember the moment itself, but you feel its echo. In your tone. In your pace. In the way your breath shortens when something familiar, but not quite right, stirs in the room. This is scar tissue, emotional, mental, even relational, and it doesn't lie. It doesn't need words. It just reacts. And unless you understand its language, you'll mistake it for instinct.

But scar tissue isn't a signal. It's residue.

It's the imprint of pain that once served as protection but now shows up uninvited. It tells you what hurt, not necessarily what's true. The job of recovery, real recovery, is learning to tell the difference.

It's surprisingly easy to conflate the two. The signal says, *This isn't safe.* The scar tissue says *this feels like what wasn't safe before.* They sound similar. But they're separated by context, and more importantly, by integration. Unprocessed experience becomes overgeneralized protection. You learn to flinch before there's impact. You say no to things that look like past threats but aren't. You call it wisdom. You tell yourself you're just being cautious. But you're not navigating the present, you're reacting to the past.

I've done this more than I care to admit. Declined opportunities that bore the shape of old wounds. Avoided people whose confidence reminded me of someone who once undermined me. Said no to collaborations because the uncertainty of shared authorship felt too close to being abandoned again. And every time, I told myself it was discernment. But it was scar tissue. It was fear dressed up as foresight.

To break that cycle, you have to get honest about what you're carrying.

Scar tissue doesn't make you weak. It makes you human. But it can also make you rigid. The very thing that once allowed you to survive becomes the thing that dulls your responsiveness. You start defending against things that aren't attacking. You assume the worst not because you're pessimistic, but because the cost of being wrong again feels unbearable.

That's the challenge. When you've lived through uncertainty, real, destabilizing, soul-level uncertainty, your nervous system doesn't forget. It learns patterns of vigilance. It adapts. It develops shortcuts for safety. And while these adaptations are brilliant in crisis, they don't age well. Over time, they turn into constraints. You stop asking, *what's possible?* And start asking, *what's survivable?*

There's a cost to that.

You might never fail as dramatically again, but you also stop risking in the ways that matter. You stop trusting your capacity to repair. You become a version of yourself optimized for control, not growth.

But here's the thing no one tells you: scar tissue can be softened. It doesn't disappear, but it can become pliable. It can become context-aware. You don't erase what you lived through; you learn to carry it with sophistication. You stop treating every reminder as a warning. You learn to pause and ask: *Is this the same situation, or just a familiar feeling?*

That pause is where freedom lives.

Because now you're not just reacting, you're discerning. You can still feel the heat of the old wound, but you don't let it dictate your behavior. You recognize the difference between fear and intuition. Between discomfort and danger. Between memory and prophecy.

This takes time. And it takes gentleness. You can't bulldoze your way through old pain. You have to meet it with curiosity. You have to notice what still stings, and why. You have to let yourself grieve what could've been if you hadn't been forced to adapt so early, or so quickly, or so thoroughly. That grief doesn't paralyze; it clarifies. It reminds you that you're not weak for needing healing. You're strong for recognizing what hasn't healed.

And once you do that, you begin to hear your actual signal again. Not the static of unresolved trauma. Not the alarms of outdated defenses. But the quieter, more precise voice underneath. The one that says: *This is right for me. This is worth the risk. This is different than before.*

Reclaiming that signal is an act of self-trust.

It's how you return to choice.

Because here's the truth: your scar tissue doesn't get to decide your future. It doesn't hold the pen. It may still whisper. It may still pulse. But you can write your way forward anyway. You can learn to act even when the memory hurts. You can re-engage with uncertainty, not because it stopped being scary, but because you've stopped being scared of yourself.

There's a quiet dignity in that. In choosing not to be defined by your damage. In choosing to stay open, even after betrayal. In choosing to trust your instincts, even when they were wrong once. That's not naivety. That's wisdom tempered by complexity.

And when others see you living that way—clear-eyed, scarred, but still choosing—they feel it. Because you're not modeling perfection, you're modeling resilience. And that's what we need more of: not people with all the answers, but people who can stay present when the answers never come. You don't have to hide your scars—but you don't have to let them speak for you either. You can acknowledge the bruise without pulling away. You can learn to tell the difference between a valid signal and the echo of old pain. And you can begin again—not despite what you've been through, but because of it.

## Chapter 33: How to Win Quietly

There is a kind of victory that doesn't arrive with applause. It doesn't trend. It doesn't register in algorithms. It doesn't produce envy, or provoke gossip, or even earn recognition. And yet, it might be the most crucial win you ever experience, the one where you prove something to yourself, and no one else even knows it happened. In a world obsessed with visibility, that kind of victory almost doesn't count. But in the inner life, the place where truth outlives trend, it counts more than anything.

To win quietly is to reject the performance of success. It's to resist the impulse to narrate every move, to seek validation for each step of progress, to turn private clarity into public content. It's to leave some of your most meaningful achievements undocumented, not out of secrecy but out of sovereignty. You know you did the work. You know what it costs. You know what you carried and still managed to set down gently. And that is enough.

But the world rarely affirms this kind of restraint. Instead, it tempts us to announce ourselves. Every milestone is an opportunity to post. Every insight becomes a thread. Every transition becomes a brand story. And slowly, without meaning to, we start measuring our growth by its reception. We tether the worth of our evolution to the feedback it garners. We lose the distinction between being seen and being whole.

Winning quietly, then, is a kind of rebellion. It's a refusal to let your journey be flattened into a highlight reel. It's the decision to protect your becoming from the corrosive glare of public performance. Not because you're hiding, but because you're building something that doesn't need permission to exist.

There's a strength in this silence that people often misunderstand. They confuse it with timidity or passivity. They assume that if you're not broadcasting your wins, you must not be winning. But those who've walked through fire don't always talk about the smoke. They breathe differently. They move differently. Their presence carries a gravity that doesn't need explanation.

The hardest part of winning quietly is resisting the urge to prove oneself, especially when the pain you overcame was dismissed, especially when your prior self was underestimated. Especially when those around you were loud about your flaws and silent about your growth. The ego wants vindication. It wants the scoreboard. It wants the people who doubted you to be forced to clap. But real maturity is when you realize: I don't need to correct their memory of me. I need to stay true to the version of myself I fought so hard to become.

This doesn't mean you never share your story. It means you choose when and how to tell it. You don't need an audience for every phase. Some growth is too sacred to live online. Some wins are meant to remain yours alone, not because they're small, but because they're formative. Because to share them prematurely would be to dilute their power, to invite commentary where you're still cultivating confidence.

Quietly winning also means learning to recalibrate your internal scoreboard. When you stop outsourcing your sense of progress to other people's metrics, you begin to redefine what success means. Sometimes the most significant win is that you didn't spiral. That you returned the text with clarity, not chaos.

That you didn't chase what you used to hunt. That you stayed instead of fleeing. Or fled instead of faking that you told the truth when a lie would've been easier. These are not viral moments. But they are revolutionary acts of alignment.

I've come to believe that every season of fundamental transformation needs at least one win that you don't share. A moment that belongs only to you. A decision you make with no external reward. A boundary you set that no one witnesses, but changes everything. These moments don't build your brand. They develop your backbone.

And yet, there's a loneliness to this. Not because you're disconnected, but because few people are trained to celebrate this kind of victory. Our culture struggles to handle subtlety. We like our growth to be visible and monetized. We want our wins to be marketable. But the most important parts of a person's transformation often happen in obscurity. In kitchens. In quiet car rides. In the spaces where no one's looking, and that's precisely why something true can finally emerge.

To win quietly is also to honor the cost. Because some victories are messy, they come with grief. They mark the end of an old self, an old dream, an old version of who you thought you had to be. And it's hard to package that. There's no tidy caption for walking away from something that looked like success to everyone else but felt like death to you. There's no easy language for explaining that the best thing you ever did was also the hardest.

But in time, you learn that silence isn't emptiness, it's integrity. It's the space between action and applause where you build an unshakeable sense of self. And in that space, something profound happens. You stop waiting to be chosen. You stop waiting for your win to be ratified. You no longer need others to see it to know it's real.

This isn't a call to be invisible. It's a call to be whole. To know the difference between sharing from abundance and sharing from a need to be affirmed. To reserve the right to evolve without broadcasting every iteration. To claim the right to succeed without explanation.

When the time comes, when you cross that invisible finish line, when you make the call you once feared, when you notice that you've become the kind of person you used to look up to, pause. Don't rush to narrate. Please don't turn it into a lesson. Just feel it. Let the win land. Let it settle into your bones.

Then keep going.

Because some of the loudest lives are the hollowest, and some of the quietest lives are the most complete.

# Chapter 34: Contingency Sovereignty

You don't truly understand your relationship with uncertainty until your Plan A begins to unravel. It's one thing to claim adaptability when things go your way. It's another entirely to watch your first idea collapse, your original timeline evaporate, or your chosen path become blocked, and still maintain a sense of agency. This is where most people stall. Not because they lack options, but because they never learned how to hold power when certainty exists in the room.

There's a common but dangerous belief that having a backup plan is a form of hesitance. By preparing for alternatives, you're essentially inviting failure into the room. That conviction and contingency cannot coexist. But in practice, this dichotomy collapses. The people who move through chaos most effectively are rarely the ones with a single, fixed plan; they're the ones who know what to do when the ground shifts. And they know it not because they're lucky, but because they've made sovereignty their baseline. They do not surrender authorship just because conditions change.

Contingency sovereignty is the ability to retain directional power even when outcomes are out of your control. It is not simply risk management, though that's a piece of it. It is a deeper stance, a psychological infrastructure that allows you to change plans without changing posture. Without collapsing into panic. Without outsourcing your decisions to the most convenient authority. Without scrambling to find someone to blame. Contingency sovereignty is what keeps you in the driver's seat when the GPS starts speaking in riddles.

And make no mistake, uncertainty will always require rerouting. No map, no matter how carefully drawn, survives contact with reality. There will be fog. There will be wrong turns. There will be delayed flights, missed signals, and abrupt endings. And if your only orientation is linear progress, you'll find yourself emotionally stranded the moment the path becomes nonlinear.

I've experienced this firsthand in ways that humbled me. There were moments when I overcommitted to a narrative that no longer served the moment. When I thought stubbornness was strength. When I mistook rigidity for loyalty to the plan, and in those moments, I didn't just lose time, I lost trust in myself. Because the deeper cost of denying uncertainty isn't delay, it's disorientation. When you override your sense that something has changed, you begin to erode your internal compass. You start second-guessing not just the plan, but your ability to respond when the plan stops working.

That's the turning point. Because when you reclaim your right to pivot without apology, everything starts to loosen. The pressure to be right dissolves. The fear of appearing inconsistent fades. You stop narrating your decisions through the lens of audience approval. You stop trying to predict every outcome and instead start preparing your presence. You begin to orient not around control, but around clarity.

To do this well, you need more than just fallback options. You need fallback *values*. You need to know not just what to do, but what matters most when everything is in flux. Is it transparency? Is it speed? Is it protecting relationships over revenue? Is it truth over tempo? Without this clarity, your contingency plans become reactive instead of responsive. They become a scramble rather than a strategy.

Contingency sovereignty also requires a kind of ego untangling. Because sometimes, the plan that needs to change is the one you were most proud of. Sometimes, the timeline that needs to be extended is the one you promised publicly. And sometimes, the team that needs to step back is the one you handpicked. These adjustments sting, not because they're wrong, but because they bruise the identity you built around being certain. Around being correct. Around being the one with the answer.

But you can't lead well, and you certainly can't live well, if your identity is anchored to infallibility.

To step into contingency sovereignty is to decide that resilience matters more than righteousness. That agility is not betrayal. That being the kind of person who can hold the wheel in a storm is more valuable than being the kind of person who never gets caught in one.

I've seen people freeze in moments when they needed to bend. I've seen leaders cling to outdated strategies because admitting the change felt like failure. I've seen creatives abandon great ideas because the first draft didn't land. I've seen partnerships dissolve not because there was no future, but because no one was willing to reimagine it. All of it comes down to the same mistake: we confuse consistency with coherence.

But the truth is, coherence often requires deviation. Sometimes the most aligned path forward looks nothing like the one you mapped out. And sometimes, the most honest answer you can offer is: *The plan changed, and here's what we're doing now.*

If you can say that without shame, you're not just surviving uncertainty, you're leading through it.

There's a dignity to that. And there's a relief, too. Because when you know you're allowed to pivot, your plans become playgrounds instead of prisons. You stop fearing failure as a final verdict. You begin to hold ambition and adaptability in the same hand. And that's where real power lives, not in the illusion of perfect foresight, but in the practiced art of continuous reorientation.

So if you're building something, anything, a business, a book, a new way of living, ask yourself not just *What's the plan?* But what *happens when this doesn't go as planned?* Who are you then? What do you reach for? How quickly can you return to center? What's your protocol, not just for execution, but for recovery?

Because sovereignty in uncertainty isn't about eliminating surprise, it's about knowing who you are in the middle of one.

It's not about staying the course no matter what. It's about knowing when the course no longer serves the destination and having the clarity and courage to adjust without apology.

That's not a backup plan. That's leadership.

# Chapter 35: The Compass and the Compass Only

In a world overwhelmed by noise, data, and the relentless demand for optimization, the simplest tool often becomes the hardest to trust: your internal compass. We've been conditioned to seek certainty externally, through experts, algorithms, metrics, and consensus, but the more profound truth is that your most reliable guide lives inside you. The compass you carry, if you listen closely, can navigate you through the fog that no map or forecast can penetrate.

The compass doesn't promise a straight line. It doesn't guarantee a smooth journey. It whispers direction, not destination. And it requires calibration, a constant tending to your values, your instincts, and your lived experience. Without that maintenance, it can spin wildly, leading you astray or paralyzing you with indecision.

I learned the power of this compass the hard way. Early in my career, I relied heavily on external validation. I chased plans because they were approved, strategies because they were popular, decisions because they were safe. But the more I did that, the more I felt disconnected, not just from my work, but from myself. I had tools, yes, but no sense of direction.

It was only when I started to listen inward that I began to find coherence. Not in certainty, but in alignment. Not in clarity of outcome, but in clarity of intention. The compass asks: *What matters most here? What can I live with? What does this choice say about who I want to be?* And those are questions no spreadsheet can answer.

The compass is deeply personal. Your history, your scars, your triumphs, and your fears shape it. It's not infallible; it can be clouded by bias, doubt, or exhaustion, but it's uniquely yours. The challenge is to learn when to trust it and when to question it without abandoning it.

One of the hardest lessons I learned was that the compass doesn't always point to the popular path. Sometimes it leads you into solitude. Sometimes it asks you to say no when yes is expected. Sometimes it pushes you to abandon plans that others still champion. And that can feel isolating. But that's the price of proper alignment. The cost of staying true is often social discomfort, professional risk, and internal vulnerability.

But the alternative, living by the noise, by the maps made for others, is a slow disintegration. It's a life lived in contradiction. You achieve milestones but feel disconnected. You collect accolades but lose coherence. You move fast but lose your center.

The compass isn't a shortcut. It's a commitment. A discipline. A relationship that requires honesty and courage. You have to be willing to admit when you're lost, to recalibrate without shame, to accept uncertainty without panic. You have to learn to hold the paradox of knowing that you don't know, while still moving forward.

Calibration happens in the quiet moments. In reflection. In solitude. In conversation with trusted others who don't drown out your signal. It happens when you pause to notice your body's response to choices, your heart's resonance with possibilities, your mind's clarity or confusion. And it deepens when you learn to integrate past lessons without being trapped by them.

In this way, the compass is both a tool and a teacher. It guides you forward, but it also teaches you how to navigate on your own. How to balance ambition with acceptance, risk with caution, action with patience. It's the place where strategy meets soul.

I don't want to romanticize this. The compass can falter. You can misread it. You can follow it into dead ends or traps. But that's part of the journey. The compass isn't about perfection. It's about presence. About learning to listen deeply, to course-correct as needed, and to carry your sense of direction when everything else is uncertain.

To trust your compass is to claim sovereignty over your path. It's to say: *No matter what storms come, I have an anchor.* It doesn't make you immune to chaos, but it makes you resilient to it. And resilience is the real win in a world that can't promise safety.

If you find yourself overwhelmed by options, drowned in advice, or paralyzed by data, pause. Take a breath. Return inward. Find your compass, not in a moment of desperation, but as a daily practice. Because when the noise grows loud and the future feels unstable, that internal guide is the one thing you can always rely on.

# Chapter 36: Teaching Others to Navigate the Fog

Navigating uncertainty is often described as a solitary journey, but it rarely is. Whether we acknowledge it or not, we pass through the fog alongside others, mentors, peers, sometimes strangers, each carrying their maps and markers, their scars and signals. But the accurate measure of mastery in uncertainty isn't just how well you manage your path; it's how you help others find their footing when the terrain shifts beneath their feet.

Teaching others to navigate the fog is a delicate art. It's not about handing out definitive answers or safe routes. It's about cultivating capacity, building muscle memory for discomfort, tolerance for ambiguity, and confidence in incomplete information. It's about preparing others to move forward without perfect clarity, to stay present without certainty, and to trust themselves even when the horizon dissolves.

I've had the privilege of guiding many through moments of chaos and transition. Some came to me expecting formulas, checklists, and guarantees. What they left with was often something less tangible but infinitely more powerful: permission to be uncertain. Permission to ask questions without needing immediate answers. Permission to fail without shame. Permission to pause, reflect, and then act again.

This work requires humility. As a teacher, you must accept that you cannot shield others from uncertainty. You cannot hand them a map that never changes or a compass that never wavers. What you can offer is presence. A steady hand. A shared language for navigating the unknown. And, most importantly, a model of resilience in the face of not-knowing.

There's a tendency to want to protect others from the discomfort of uncertainty, to offer false certainty as a balm. But doing so does a disservice. It teaches dependency rather than autonomy. It fosters fear rather than courage. Actual teaching in this domain is about creating environments where exploration is safe, where mistakes are expected, and where the journey itself is valued over the destination.

That's a tough message to convey in cultures obsessed with outcomes and efficiency. We want progress to be linear, growth to be measurable, and success to be apparent. But uncertainty resists those neat boxes. It thrives in the cracks, the detours, the questions without answers. To teach others to navigate this fog, you must also be willing to sit with discomfort. To stay curious when confusion arises. To normalize doubt as a companion rather than an enemy.

One of the most powerful tools I've found in this work is storytelling. Sharing your own experiences of uncertainty, including failures and moments of vulnerability, breaks down the illusion of mastery. It humanizes the process. It reminds others that they're not alone. That even those who seem steady and sure have wrestled with shadows.

But beyond stories, teaching requires trust. Trust that others will find their way, even if it looks different from yours. Trust that your role is not to dictate but to guide, not to answer but to question. Trust that the best lessons come from lived experience, from trial and error, from the messy dance between hope and fear.

And trust in timing. Some people are ready to navigate the fog sooner than others. Some need more time, more space, more failure before they find their stride. Teaching isn't about rushing anyone. It's about holding a container for growth at its own pace.

I've seen this approach transform teams, organizations, and families. It changes the culture from one of control to one of learning. From one of compliance to one of curiosity. From one of fear to one of resilience.

The greatest gift you can give someone in uncertainty is the courage to be themselves in the storm. To hold their ground without needing to know all the answers. To keep moving even when the way isn't clear.

Because navigating the fog is less about avoiding mistakes and more about learning how to course-correct. Less about finding perfect certainty and more about embracing the journey as it unfolds.

In teaching others to navigate the fog, you're not just passing on knowledge; you're passing on freedom.

And in a world that often feels like it's unraveling, that freedom is revolutionary.

# Chapter 37: Decentralized Wisdom

Wisdom is often thought of as the product of singular insight, a solitary moment of clarity born from deep reflection or intense experience. But in an age defined by complexity, interconnectedness, and rapid change, wisdom rarely belongs to one mind alone. Instead, it emerges from the collective. It is decentralized, distributed across networks, communities, and systems that learn and adapt together.

Decentralized wisdom acknowledges a fundamental truth about uncertainty: no single person, no matter how talented or experienced, can hold all the answers. The terrain is too vast, the variables too many, and the future too mutable. What matters, then, is not individual genius but collective intelligence. The ability to tap into diverse perspectives, to synthesize conflicting information, and to co-create adaptive strategies in real time.

I've seen the power of decentralized wisdom in practice many times. In teams that cultivate psychological safety, dissent is welcomed rather than feared. In communities that honor lived experience alongside expertise. In organizations that build feedback loops into every layer of decision-making, they can foster a culture of continuous improvement. These groups don't just react to uncertainty; they anticipate it, surf it, and sometimes even shape it.

But building decentralized wisdom isn't easy. It requires humility. A willingness to let go of control. An embrace of ambiguity not just as a condition to endure, but as a resource to harness. It challenges traditional hierarchies that equate authority with knowledge and instead values the distributed flow of information and insight.

This shift can be disorienting for leaders trained in command-and-control models. It demands new skills: listening more than speaking, asking better questions than giving answers, and creating space for voices that were previously marginalized. It also requires patience, because collective wisdom develops slowly, through trust-building, experimentation, and sometimes failure.

One of the most valuable lessons I've learned is that decentralized wisdom doesn't mean consensus. It means connection. It's not about everyone agreeing, but about everyone being heard and valued. It's the art of holding multiple truths at once, balancing competing priorities, and moving forward with a patchwork of confidence and caution.

In practice, this often looks messy. Conversations that circle back. Decisions that are revisited. Strategies that evolve. But beneath the apparent chaos is a dynamic equilibrium, a system that is both robust and flexible, capable of adapting faster than any individual could alone.

Decentralized wisdom also democratizes responsibility. When everyone is invited to contribute, everyone becomes a steward of uncertainty. The burden of decision-making is shared, reducing burnout and enhancing resilience. It creates a culture where failure is a collective learning opportunity, not an individual shame.

I remember working with a startup navigating a sudden market shift. Instead of defaulting to top-down edicts, the leadership opened the floor. Teams from product, marketing, customer support, and operations gathered in cross-functional huddles. They shared data, hypotheses, and fears. They surfaced assumptions and tested ideas. Over weeks, this decentralized approach produced strategies that were more nuanced, adaptable, and widely supported than anything a single leader could have crafted alone.

This is the future of decision-making in uncertain times. It's less about certainty and more about connection. Less about the lone hero and more about the networked node. Less about control and more about cultivation.

For those who lead in this new paradigm, the role shifts from commander to gardener, from dictating outcomes to nurturing conditions where wisdom can grow. It's a humbling role, but also a deeply rewarding one.

Decentralized wisdom doesn't promise easy answers. It promises resilience. It promises agility. It promises the capacity to keep learning when the path forward is unclear.

And in a world that's more volatile, uncertain, complex, and ambiguous than ever before, that capacity might be the most significant advantage of all.

# Chapter 38: Legacy-Level Decisions

Most decisions are small. What to eat for dinner? Which email should I respond to first? When to schedule a meeting. But some decisions carry a weight that transcends the immediate moment. They ripple across years, generations, even centuries. These are legacy-level decisions, the kind that shape not just your life, but the lives of people you may never meet. They demand a type of thinking and responsibility unlike any other.

Legacy-level decisions confront us with uncertainty on a scale that can be paralyzing. The stakes are vast, the variables complex, and the consequences long-lasting. And yet, we are called to make them. Leaders, parents, creators, citizens, each of us will face moments when the choices before us are not just about personal gain or survival, but about the kind of world we want to leave behind.

I've grappled with these decisions more than once. The choice to step away from a role that no longer aligned with my values. The decision to invest in projects with uncertain returns but the potential for a profound impact. The moments when I had to weigh immediate comfort against long-term integrity. Each brought its kind of fog, a kind of uncertainty that no amount of data could fully resolve.

Legacy-level decisions require a different kind of clarity. Not the clarity of certainty or predictability, but the clarity of purpose. A deep sense of what matters most, beyond the noise of the moment. They call for a vision that stretches beyond the horizon, tempered by humility about what we can control.

These decisions also demand patience. Because legacy is built over time, it cannot be rushed or forced. It requires consistency, yes, but also adaptability. The willingness to course-correct while holding the core values steady. It's a dance between steadfastness and flexibility, between ambition and acceptance.

One of the hardest lessons I've learned is that legacy is less about grand gestures and more about daily actions. The way you show up when no one is watching. The decisions you make in quiet moments. The integrity you maintain in the small things. Legacy is accumulated character, not headline achievements.

This perspective changes how you approach risk. You become less focused on avoiding failure and more focused on preventing compromise. Less concerned with short-term gains and more committed to long-term alignment. It's a shift from playing to win to playing to be remembered well.

Legacy-level decisions also require courage. The courage to stand alone when necessary. To make unpopular choices. To accept that your impact might not be visible in your lifetime. To carry the weight of uncertainty without succumbing to despair.

I've witnessed leaders who faltered because they sought approval over authenticity. I've seen creators abandon projects too soon because the results weren't immediate. I've watched families fracture over decisions made in haste or fear. All of these are reminders that legacy is fragile and demands careful stewardship.

But I've also seen the opposite. People who commit to legacy-level decisions with a quiet resolve that inspires others. Who lead not with loud declarations but with consistent integrity. Those who embrace uncertainty as part of their responsibility. Who plants seeds they may never see bloom.

That kind of leadership is rare. It's demanding. But it's also profoundly rewarding because it connects you to something beyond yourself. Something enduring. Something that outlives the chaos and noise of the present.

So when you face legacy-level decisions, remember this: you are not alone. The weight you carry is shared across time and space—the choices you make echo in ways you cannot yet see. And the best you can do is approach them with clarity, courage, and compassion.

Legacy is not a burden. It's a privilege.

# Chapter 39: The Anti-FOMO Framework

Fear of missing out, or FOMO, is a modern affliction that gnaws at our sense of satisfaction and presence. It's the anxiety that someone, somewhere, is living a better, fuller, more exciting life than we are. Social media fuels it with highlight reels, endless notifications, and the curated stories of success that flood our screens. But FOMO isn't just a cultural phenomenon; it's a symptom of a deeper struggle with uncertainty, scarcity, and identity.

The Anti-FOMO Framework is not about chasing more or trying to be everywhere at once. It's about reclaiming your attention, your values, and your time in a world designed to fragment both. It's a deliberate practice to resist the pull of distraction and comparison, and instead cultivate focus, contentment, and intentionality.

At its core, the framework acknowledges that you will always miss things. You can't be everywhere or do everything. That's not failure, that's reality. The question isn't how to avoid missing out, but how to choose what matters deeply so that missing the rest becomes a source of peace, not panic.

Building this framework starts with clarity. Clarity about your priorities, your goals, and your limits. When you know what truly matters, the noise of what doesn't begins to fade. You develop filters, not just for information, but for invitation and expectation. You learn to say no without guilt, to protect your boundaries with kindness, and to recognize that every yes to one thing is a no to something else.

This is hard work. The cultural current pushes in the opposite direction. It tells you to seize every opportunity, to maximize your network, to curate your brand constantly. It equates busyness with value, visibility with worth, and growth with identity. The Anti-FOMO Framework challenges all of that. It asks: What if less is more? What if depth is better than breadth? What if your presence, not your popularity, is your greatest asset?

Practicing this framework requires both courage and compassion. Courage to resist the lure of social comparison and the fear of exclusion. Compassion for yourself when you slip into old habits of distraction or overcommitment. It's a continuous dance of awareness and adjustment.

One of the most powerful tools in this work is ritual. Rituals anchor you in what matters. They create sacred space for focus and reflection. They remind you daily who you are beyond the noise. Whether it's a morning routine, a weekly pause, or a digital Sabbath, rituals form the scaffolding of resistance.

The framework also embraces imperfection. You won't always succeed in staying centered. There will be moments of doubt, anxiety, and distraction. That's normal. The goal isn't to eliminate FOMO; it's to build resilience so that when it arises, it doesn't derail you.

I've seen this framework transform lives. People who once felt overwhelmed and scattered begin to find rhythm and peace. They stop chasing trends and start chasing meaning. They learn to inhabit their own space fully, rather than constantly looking over their shoulder.

In a world that thrives on FOMO, the Anti-FOMO Framework is revolutionary. It's a declaration that you will not be defined by what you miss, but by what you choose to embrace. It's a commitment to presence over performance, to intention over impulse.

If you feel the pull, the anxiety of omission, the pressure to be everywhere, know that you can reclaim your power. You can build a framework that supports focus, clarity, and peace. And in doing so, you'll find that missing out on the rest isn't a loss, it's liberation.

# Chapter 40: The Quiet Pivot

Not every transformation arrives with fanfare. Not every shift demands a spotlight. Sometimes, the most profound changes happen in silence, when you stop pushing against the current and let yourself drift into a new flow. That is the quiet pivot. It is a subtle, unannounced course correction that feels less like a declaration and more like a deep sigh of relief.

The quiet pivot is different from dramatic reinvention. It doesn't require a manifesto or a public commitment. It doesn't come with grand gestures or bold statements. Instead, it's a steady, often invisible realignment, a recalibration of values, priorities, and identity that slowly reshapes your trajectory.

I've learned to respect these moments. They often arrive when the noise of urgency finally fades, when exhaustion makes bravado impossible, when you've reached a threshold of honesty that can't be ignored. The quiet pivot isn't about giving up; it's about giving in, to what's real, to what's sustainable, to what feels authentic.

In a culture that celebrates rapid change and visible breakthroughs, the quiet pivot can be misunderstood. It can feel like stagnation or defeat to those watching from the outside. But those who live it know it's anything but. It's a form of survival. A practice of resilience. A statement of self-respect.

The pivot is quiet because it's humble. It acknowledges that you don't have all the answers. That the path isn't linear. That growth is often incremental and uneven. It's less about proving yourself and more about proving to yourself that you can hold complexity without collapse.

The quiet pivot is also deeply strategic. Because it allows you to conserve energy, build capacity, and prepare for what's next without burning out. It's the art of slowing down to speed up, of stepping back to move forward with more intention.

I've made many quiet pivots in my life. Sometimes they felt like minor course corrections, changing the focus of a project, shifting my daily routine, reevaluating a relationship. Other times, they were seismic, deciding to leave a career path, moving cities, and redefining what success meant to me. But in all cases, these pivots carried a common thread: they were driven by an internal signal that was louder than external expectations.

Listening to that signal takes courage. It means trusting yourself when no one else does. It means valuing your own experience over popular opinion. It means accepting that growth often looks quiet, confusing, and ambiguous.

But it also means that the pivot is sustainable. It's less likely to be followed by burnout or regret. It's more likely to lead to a life that feels whole, coherent, and true.

The quiet pivot invites you to embrace uncertainty not as a problem to solve, but as a condition to live with. It reminds you that stability isn't about static conditions but about adaptability. That strength isn't always visible but is often found in endurance.

And perhaps most importantly, the quiet pivot offers a different kind of victory. One that doesn't require applause. One that isn't dependent on recognition. One that is its reward.

As you close this book and step back into your life, I invite you to consider where a quiet pivot might be waiting for you, where you might stop trying to force the narrative and instead allow it to unfold, where you might stop chasing certainty and start honoring your rhythm.

Because living well with uncertainty isn't about conquering it, it's about dancing with it. Sometimes loudly, sometimes quietly. And always, with intention.

# Epilogue

# High-Stakes Living in a Low-Stakes World

We live in a world that constantly tells us not to take things too seriously. That life is a game, a show, a fleeting moment to be enjoyed or endured. That risk is something to be minimized, discomfort to be avoided, and failure to be hidden.

But high-stakes living, true high-stakes living, is something else entirely. It's the choice to engage deeply, to care fiercely, to decide with courage even when the outcomes are unknowable. It's the refusal to shrink in the face of uncertainty, and the commitment to move forward anyway.

This book has taken you through the shadows and light of uncertainty, showing that fear is not a barrier but a guide. That the unknown is not a void but a space rich with possibility. That resilience is not about armor but about openness.

In a culture that promotes distraction and superficiality, living with high stakes requires radical attention. It asks you to be present, to be authentic, to be accountable, not just to others, but to yourself. It means carrying the weight of your choices without surrendering your freedom. It means navigating complexity with humility and conviction.

High-stakes living doesn't promise safety or success. It promises presence and agency. It asks you to be both brave and wise, to hold tension without breaking, to trust yourself when the path is unclear.

And that trust is the most powerful lever of all.

As you move forward, remember: the world may urge you to take the easy route, to settle for certainty, to avoid discomfort. But your life is yours to lead. To decide. To risk. To craft with intention.

Embrace the high stakes. Surf the uncertainty. Live fully, because the only absolute failure is to shrink from the challenge of being alive.

The tide is not waiting. The wave is rising. Will you stand ready?

# About the Author

Oliver Bennett is a seasoned writer and thinker who has spent decades exploring the subtle dynamics of decision-making, resilience, and navigating uncertainty. Writing under this British pen name, Oliver combines deep research, lived experience, and a commitment to honest storytelling to illuminate how individuals can find clarity amid chaos.

Oliver's work in *The Book On* series has reached thousands of readers worldwide, helping them rethink risk, long-term thinking, and strategic living with nuance and rigor. Known for a sharp, engaging narrative style, Oliver writes to challenge complacency and invite readers into a more intentional way of living.

Away from the page, Oliver is passionate about empowering others to embrace uncertainty as a source of strength and growth, believing that the most significant leverage lies in learning to surf life's inevitable waves.

# About The Publisher

Welcome to The Book On Publishing

At The Book On Publishing, we believe in rewriting the rules of learning. Whether you're chasing your next big idea, building a better life, or simply curious about what should have been taught in school, you've come to the right place.

We're a platform built for dreamers, doers, and lifelong learners, offering bold, practical books and tools that empower you to take charge of your journey. From real-world skills to mindset mastery, we publish the book on what matters.

No fluff. No lectures. Just what you need to know, delivered with clarity, purpose, and a spark of curiosity.

Start exploring. Start growing. Start writing your story.

Read more at https://thebookon.ca.

# Acknowledgment of AI Assistance

Portions of this book were developed with the support of AI. While every word has been carefully reviewed and refined by the author, AI served as a valuable tool for brainstorming, editing, and structuring ideas. Its assistance helped accelerate the creative process and bring clarity to complex topics.

www.ingramcontent.com/pod-product-compliance
Lightning Source LLC
Chambersburg PA
CBHW071742120626
46550CB00002B/631